A Treaty Too Far

A Ne

Michael Spicer has been
Worcestershire since 1974
Conservative Party 1983/4,
1987, Minister for Coal and
Minister for Housing in 1990
in 1969 he founded an economic consultancy. He is the author
of several thrillers set in the Cotswolds.

He is currently Chairman of the Parliamentary Office of
Science and Technology and Chairman of the Association of
Independent Electricity Producers. He has a degree from
Cambridge University in Economics and is married with three
children.

A Treaty Too Far

A New Policy for Europe

Michael Spicer

FOURTH ESTATE · *London*

First published in Great Britain in 1992 by
Fourth Estate Limited
289 Westbourne Grove
London W11 2QA

Reprinted 1992

ISBN 1–85702–102–9

Typeset by York House Typographic Ltd, London
Printed in England by Clays Ltd, St Ives plc

Contents

Foreword

IREMEMBER Maastricht as a charming town where in 1982 we held a European Summit under the excellent chairmanship of the then Prime Minister of the Netherlands, Mr Van Agt. We were not able to agree a Common Fisheries Policy, which was our objective, because France was not prepared to commit herself at that time. The people were welcoming and I have always retained a great affection for the town . But I do not welcome the new Treaty that bears its name.

As the Treaty itself points out, it marks a new stage in the process of creating an ever closer union among the people of Europe. Indeed it establishes a European Union, and an Economic and Monetary Union including ultimately a single currency. It creates a citizenship of the Union with voting rights, implements a common foreign and security policy, and greatly extends the authority of the bureaucratic Commission and its period of office. Taken together these things have the attributes of a Federal state, unlike the Treaty of Rome and the Single European Act.

Michael Spicer has done us all a service in setting these great matters in the context of history, analysing them in detail and describing their effects. Everyone who has the duty of deciding whether or not to ratify the Maastricht Treaty, or who is concerned about its consequences, should read this book.

Both Disraeli and Churchill said the first duty of the Conservative Party is to uphold the constitution. The Maastricht Treaty would change it fundamentally. Britain has always been interested in what happens in Europe and has made great sacrifices of blood to restore liberty to its peoples. But we have always retained our sovereignty, our sturdy independence, sense of fairness and wider outlook on the world. All these things are reflected in our parliamentary institutions, our laws and customs.

The debate on the Treaty has often been conducted in broad general terms – some opaque, others giving misleading analogies like 'the European train leaving the station' or a 'two-speed Europe'. If that train is going in the wrong direction it is better not to be on it at all. The 'Newspeak' of Orwell has returned as 'EMUspeak'.

More and more of the peoples of Europe are becoming restless and hostile about the Maastricht Treaty. There seems to be a wide gap between some parliamentarians elected to represent the people and the people themselves. Each nation is free to say 'Yes' or 'No' to the Treaty. And there must be no criticism or coercion of those who say 'No' – *that* after all is the freedom for which we fought. Moreover each of those countries would still be a member of the Community under the Treaty of Rome and the Single European Act. We are all bound by those.

Let the debate and discussion continue to be vigorous, informed and sensitive. Do not be discomforted by any attempt to suggest that 'Maastricht' is inevitable. That's what they said about Communism.

The Rt Hon Margaret Thatcher OM FRS

Acknowledgements

I AM INDEBTED to Daniel Hannan for the help I have received in writing this book. He provided much of the research and a great deal of the drafting.

I wish also to thank Margaret Bottomley, whose assistance with the typing, presentation and the index was, as it always has been over the past quarter of a century, invaluable. A big 'thank you' also to my wife, Ann, who on this occasion, as on others, has done so much to help sort out all the mass of paper which a project such as this generates.

The publisher and I would like to thank York House Typographic and Clays Ltd who expertly typeset and printed the book at great speed, to keep pace with the daily developments of the debate.

I dedicate the book to my constituents in South Worcestershire, who have not only elected me to Parliament on six occasions but also over the past nineteen years given me so much support and encouragement. May I and my successors continue to represent their interests in a Parliament which is the sovereign authority in our land.

Michael Spicer
October 1992

Introduction

THERE ARE those who argue that the Treaty on European Union, initialled by heads of government at Maastricht in December 1991, and the disastrous course of events which has overtaken the British economy (and now threatens the other economies of Europe) are matters totally unrelated to each other, to be compartmentalised and sorted out separately. They are not. Politicians – and they include, it would seem, the collective leaderships of all Britain's main political parties – who profess to be 'horrified' by the current and seemingly worsening recession but who are at the same time in favour of Maastricht, are deluding themselves.

The events which led up to Maastricht and the philosophy which lies behind it are inextricably linked to the reversal of Britain's economic regeneration launched with such promise in the early 1980s. The linkage is the obsession with the exchange rate of the currency at the expense of policies (notably with respect to interest rates and the supply of money) geared to the requirements of the real economy. It has happened before, when the desire by the British Government (again, abetted by the Opposition front

1

bench and certain corporate interests) to link up with the Americans and to return to the Gold Standard, led to the appalling economic deprivations of the 1920s and early 1930s.

The policy of giving priority to exchange-rate management, reintroduced in Britain in the mid-1980s and formalised in the late summer of 1990 with entry into the European Exchange Rate Mechanism, was a prerequisite for signing the Treaty of Maastricht. It lurks in the background so long as 'Maastricht' remains on the table. The criteria outlined in Article 109j(I) of the Treaty (to which the British 'opt out' does not apply) make entry into the ERM a specific condition of signature. The notion of an irrevocable single currency, at the core of the Treaty of Maastricht, is that of fixed exchange rates in perpetuity.

The effect on the British economy of the policy of giving precedence to exchange rates was predictable and, as I show in Chapter 5, I predicted it as early as 1990 when I was still a member of the Government. Real rates of interest were continually raised, unemployment grew relentlessly and foreign reserves were depleted in a vain attempt to hold up the value of the pound. Speculators, far from being deterred, were drawn towards the financial killing which ultimately, inevitably and accurately they believed would be theirs.

The collapse of Britain's position within the ERM on 16 September 1992 was followed by an apparent attempt to readjust interest rates and the supply of money to suit the increasingly desperate needs of the economy.

There are, it has to be said, several reasons for believing that the impact of the change of policy (if change of policy there has been) will be long delayed and that unemployment will continue to rise, perhaps even towards the four million mark. The first is that the effect on confidence of a change in interest rates is likely, on past experience, to 'lag' by anything up to two years. It is the reason why people like me were arguing for substantive cuts in interest rates as long ago as 1990/91. Second, there remains a great deal of uncertainty about the general nature and direction of economic policy. There does not seem, for instance, to be full agreement within the Government as to whether the currently exploding level of public borrowing should be brought back under control or whether it should perhaps be increased and directed towards a socialist-type intervention to 'support' industry. Third, there is 'Maastricht'. Despite saying initially that they would wait for the Danish position to be clarified, the Government is now apparently determined to press on regardless with parliamentary ratification of the Treaty, against the wishes of two-thirds of the electorate. Maastricht, as I have said, carries with it the obligation to re-enter the ERM. The very process of signing up to Maastricht therefore undermines any efforts by the Government to release its economic policy from the constraints of exchange-rate manipulation.

It may be that the ultimate refusal of the Danish people to ratify the Treaty, or of the Germans to release control over the Deutschmark, or of the British Parliament to pass the necessary legislation, will mean that 'Maastricht' does not become law in its present form. That will not be the end of the matter.

In addition to having the potential to create the most far-reaching changes to the British constitution and to the legal system that have occurred for several centuries – some might say ever – the Maastricht Treaty is a symptom, a bench-mark, a way of thinking about Europe and about the ability within it of the nation state to survive. It assumes that events in Europe will move relentlessly and 'irrevocably' in the direction of a unified centralised state, in which responsibility is devolved through the interpretation given by the centre to the notion of 'subsidiarity'. The economic dislocation is, it is thought, a price worth paying for Federalisation.

I will have failed in my purpose in writing this book if, after I have examined and tested the Maastricht philosophy, I am not able to provide an adequate assessment of the alternative to it. One can favour the closer association of European states, as I do, without accepting the need for a single economy or for political union. There is a pressing need for an entirely different concept of what would make for harmony within Europe from that suggested by the Treaty of Maastricht.

Insofar as such a perspective has been suggested, it has usually been surrounded by pejorative vocabulary: 'fast' and 'slow' tracks. What is wrong with 'twin' tracks or even 'multiple' tracks? Why should nations which control their own economies and balance their trade in Europe with successful business in the rest of the world be thought to be anti-European? In Britain's case might not the fact that she is at the crossroads of much of world trade, moving to and from her shores, east and west as well as north and south, be a source of great commercial strength to her and therefore to her European trading partners? Might Britain's strategic trading position not explain, for instance, why she possesses the busiest and the third busiest international airports in the world? Might not the cause of the high inward investment she enjoyed in the 1980s be precisely because she spans the gulf between Europe and the Americas? There are many businessmen I know who think so. Would Britain really be on the 'fast' track if she submerged her economy and her identity with that of, for instance, Germany? If other nations see it as in their interests to join a Deutschmark area, that is for them. What is for us may be a more flexible arrangement but – at least with respect to trade and intergovernmental co-operation – no less bound into Europe.

Trade flourishes not out of uniformity but from diversity. The whole point of trade is that nations are able to swap on the back of differences. It is when a common market be-

4

comes a uniform market that trade within it begins to diminish. That may be one explanation as to why in recent years the EEC has shown relatively slow growth in trade. Is it not probable that a form of association and cooperation in Europe which is genuinely supportive of differing national interests will be far more stable and even cohesive than an arrangement whose intrinsic contradictions combined with the antipathy of the people make it at best brittle and at worst the basis for future conflict and violence?

This proposition will be fully tested in the pages that follow.

Chapter 1

Where the Laughing Stops

Until very recently, the idea that they might cease to be citizens of a sovereign state and instead owe their allegiance to a government in Brussels presiding over a United States of Europe would to most people in Britain have seemed so improbable as to be laughable.

Any change in Britain's relationships in Europe, in so far as it crossed the British consciousness at all, was about 'doing more business', buying cheap wine by the litre and 'getting together to stop another war'. More recently, it is true, the bureaucrats in Brussels seemed to have 'gone over the top' with their ideas for a Euro sausage and the right length for condoms. But the great bulk of opinion rated these, and an apparently growing number of official excesses, as being plain absurd, certainly remote, not to be taken seriously, and frankly a bit of a bore. The attitude of most of the British public remained as it had been characterised long ago by the satirical magazine *Private Eye*, on whose front cover for May 1967 there appeared the famous caption: 'Common Market: the Great Debate Begins'. It was printed under a picture of four old-age pensioners fast asleep in deckchairs. According to Gallup polls conducted in January 1985, in July 1987 and even as late as the spring of 1992, the dominant sentiment of the British public towards the EEC was one of 'indifference'.

Then came 'Maastricht'. The London *Times* said on 8 September 1992: 'Maastricht was a mistake.' It was much more than that. Whether or not the Treaty on European Union is ever brought into effect, its very existence has changed everything. It marks, for a start, the point at which those who believe in the establishment of a Federal State of Europe broke cover. Chancellor Kohl of Germany expressed it thus, before the Bertelsmann Forum (at the Petersburg Hotel, 3 April 1992):

> In Maastricht we laid the foundation-stone for the completion of the European Union. The European Union Treaty introduces a new and decisive stage in the process of European union which within a few years will lead to the creation of what the founder fathers of modern Europe dreamed of following the last war: the United States of Europe.

Despite the fact that very few people have read the 'Maastricht Treaty', the general thrust of its contents has begun slowly to percolate into the public consciousness. In Britain at least, this has prompted a general unease that 'all is not quite right' with what is happening in Europe. By 7 September 1992, 76 per cent of the British public had decided, according to an ICM poll, that they did not want to 'exchange sovereignty for closer ties with Europe'. By 5 October 1992, the eve of the Conservative Party Conference, MORI was registering 68 per cent of those polled as being 'against Maastricht'. The comparable figures in June and September had been 46 per cent and 48 per cent.

Whether or not the Treaty ever comes into effect, it has

7

left an indelible mark. People have been put on the alert, at least to the extent that they are prepared for the first time to ask the question: Where do we really want to go from here?

'The Treaty on European Union', to give it its full and accurate title, was agreed and initialled by Heads of Government on 10 December 1991. Formal signature by foreign ministers followed on 7 February 1992. Much to the consternation of all the governments concerned, it remains very far from being ratified. The primary reason for this is that in a referendum on 2 June 1992 the Government of Denmark failed to get the necessary supporting popular majority. Whatever may be said to the contrary, the Danish veto is absolute, unless another referendum were to reverse the effect of the first. There certainly does not exist the necessary five-sixths majority in the Danish Parliament to overthrow the result of the referendum.

The working of the Treaty of Rome makes the present state of impasse clear beyond peradventure. Article 236 of the Treaty of Rome reads:

> The amendments [to the Treaty] shall enter into force after being ratified by all Member States in accordance with their respective constitutional requirements.

The Maastricht Treaty on European Union comprises a set of amendments to the Treaty of Rome. By the terms of the original treaty, the Danish vote has therefore placed Maastricht in a state of suspended animation.

It is arguable that had it not been for the Danish referendum, the process of ratification of the Treaty would have been all but completed before the general public throughout Europe had any real idea of what was going on. Certainly in Britain the details of the Treaty dribbled out very slowly indeed. Members of Parliament themselves had to fight for a draft of the Treaty to be placed in the House of

Commons Library before it was debated on 19 December 1991. As for the general public, they were deprived of the text of the Treaty until five months after it had been first initialled. When it finally emerged on the streets of Britain it did so at a price of £13.30 and was only available, at least in its official form, from Her Majesty's Stationery Office. The text of this document was different, in both appearance and content, from the draft Treaty which had emerged in the House of Commons Library before Christmas. As an example, the word 'jurisdiction' (Article 3B in the earlier document) had been freely interchanged with 'competence' in the final document. The fact that competence has a different meaning from 'jurisdiction' might not matter so much were the context, for instance, a joint governmental pronouncement. Amendments to the Treaty of Rome, if ratified, are much more than agreements between governments; they become part, some would say the dominant part, of the law of the land.

In delaying the publication of the final text of the Treaty on European Union, in effectively restricting its accessibility and in publishing it in a form which is hard for the layman to follow, the British Government seemed to be heeding the advice of the French Socialist Member of the European Parliament, Jean-Pierre Cot, when he said, 'It is a mistake to let people read the Treaty; they will only misunderstand it.'

Despite this coyness of the British authorities, the Danish hiatus has given time for the implications of the Maastricht Treaty to sink into the public consciousness. There is evidence from both Britain and other countries that the very existence of the Treaty has begun to make people sit up and take note.

Not many people may have actually had the opportunity of reading Article 8, which states that 'Citizenship of the Union is hereby established . . . Citizens of the Union shall enjoy the rights conferred by this Treaty and shall be subject to the duties imposed hereby.' But increasingly

9

throughout the second half of 1992 it would seem that there were more and more people who had at least met someone who knew someone who had read these words. Nor has it apparently proved difficult, from this indirect contact with the Treaty, for people to have begun to form a firm judgement about it. Put in its most neutral form, they are not of the view that accepting the 'duties' of 'Union Citizenship' is what they had been led to believe the Common Market was all about.

I have to say it is not what I thought it was all about either. I grew up politically during the period of the European dream, when indeed it was more of a vision than a reality. In the 1960s I helped to write pamphlets calling for the permanent end to all conflict in Europe, for the creation of harmonious trading relationships, even for closer co-operation on defence. As a Member of Parliament I fought in the 1975 referendum for a 'Yes' vote for Britain's continued membership of the Common Market. From the Cotswolds to the Malvern Hills I let them have it straight in every village hall throughout the length and breadth of my constituency of South Worcestershire: what was bad for the Soviet Union was good for Britain and there was nothing the Soviet Union desired less on its doorstep, I argued, than a closely united association of free trading nations. It was not the only argument that I used, but as far as I remember it was the one I liked best.

So what has happened since those days when the people of not only Worcestershire but of the entire country voted overwhelmingly in favour of Britain's active participation in an increasingly united Europe?

The landscape has changed, certainly. The Soviet Union is no more: gone is the immediate threat to the eastern borders of Europe from a neo-imperialistic power (though no one can foretell what relations will emerge with the new Russia). Germany has become a single country of nearly one hundred million people with an economy almost as large as those of Britain and France put together; questions have arisen as to whether this means that a United Europe will inevitably have to operate under German management.

Nor has the Common Market lived up to some of the early expectations for it. Despite the removal of most of the tariff barriers between its members, the joint rate of growth of their economies has been relatively slow, at least compared with those of countries in south-east Asia. A 'single', fully competitive market was meant to have been established by the end of 1992. Indeed, this was the major justification for the very considerable extra powers given to Community institutions by the Single European Act of 1986. And yet airlines do not fly competitively between and within the Member countries; financial institutions do not trade freely across borders; producers of energy are prevented by nationalised monopolies from building competitive power stations and linking these to the local grids; the state monopolies themselves continue to receive large dollops of subsidy. It is not quite what I imagined the Common Market would turn out to be thirty-five years on.

These are all no doubt necessary (but not, I suspect, sufficient) conditions for explaining the angst, the deep melancholy, which is spreading throughout Europe about the course which events are taking in the Continent. Maastricht has exposed something beyond the failings of the market, something more profound than concerns about imbalances within the Community. It has revealed that which people may have suspected existed but which had previously been allowed to fester, out of sight, beneath the surface of political events. Maastricht began to make people wonder, most for the first time in their lives, whether nationhood had any future at all.

The process of undermining the nation state began, no doubt innocently and with benign intent, soon after the last world war, as a refinement of a move for greater friendship

11

between nations. Somewhere along the line, the ideal of amity became confused with the concept of merging identities. In my younger days, I was as guilty as others of failing to make clear the distinction. Gradually there arose amongst the rulers of Europe the notion that the nation state was at best no longer relevant and at worst the source of much that was evil in international affairs. History came to be written, at least in part, so that European wars were described as having been attributable solely to rivalry between nations rather than to dictators who with their totalitarian ideologies had broken asunder evidently fragile democratic structures.

At the intergovernmental conferences which preceded the Maastricht Treaty, this mood began to emerge into the open. With the signing of the Treaty, the proposition that in Europe at least nationhood was dead or dying was revealed to have entered the mainstream of political thinking. It is in this sense that I say that Maastricht was the point at which those who espouse the cause of a Federalist European state broke cover and exposed the objective which for so long and with growing impatience they had been disguising. It is important to be clear about the precise significance of Maastricht. It is not, for instance, entirely dependent on what now happens to the Treaty. Whatever the eventual fate of this particular text, its very creation is what counts. Whether it is eventually ratified or not, Maastricht has let the Federalist cat out of the bag. Until it is superseded, it will remain the bench-mark against which the federalists will judge progress.

The 'rights' and 'wrongs' of nationhood – whether the sovereignty of national Parliaments and the allegiance of the citizens to a single country are still relevant, or whether the nations of Europe should continue to be represented in the great councils of the world, the United Nations, the IMF and so on, through their own ambassadors – are matters which can wait for later discussion. For the present, I am concerned only to be certain about the significance of what was done at Maastricht in terms of the attitude it exposes to the idea of nationhood.

The British Presidency's official leaflets about the Treaty describe it as 'checking the centralising trend'. In justification of this view, mention is made of such words as 'subsidiarity', 'limits to competence' and 'compliance with legal obligations'. It is not necessary, however, to become bogged down with the jargon of the Treaty to work out its real meaning. As a matter of fact, one word will do. Leave aside for a moment the 'duties' of the Union Citizen under Article 8 and consider this sentence under Article 3A. Referring to the proposed new economic structure, it says: 'These activities shall include the irrevocable fixing of exchange rates leading to the introduction of a single currency.'

It is the word 'irrevocable' which catches my eye. 'Irrevocable' means unalterable, gone beyond recall, in other words, for ever. It is impossible, in my view, to exaggerate the significance of the inclusion of this notion of eternity into the provisions of the Maastricht Treaty. It is what sets Maastricht apart from everything that has gone before. If it were to be ratified it would, indeed, quite literally be the point of no return.

In the United Kingdom it would have the profoundest possible consequences for the very foundations of the constitution. This rests above all on the notion that the people exert their sovereignty through a Parliament which is the supreme authority in the land. An essential element of this supremacy is that Parliament can effect whatever changes it chooses, including, often especially, amending the laws passed by a previous Parliament. The commitment at Maastricht to the 'irrevocable' is in direct contradiction to this. However, the fact is that the irrevocable powers have not yet been transferred, and sovereignty is an absolute: you either have final authority or you do not. (I have never

13

been able to understand the ideal of 'pooling sovereignty'.) In this sense, Maastricht is a torpedo aimed but not yet fired at the keel of British democracy.

Nor is the matter of what it is proposed to make irrevocable a trivial one. Indeed, it is itself a central issue in determining the future nature of the nation state in Europe.

'Irrevocable' exchange rates leading to a single currency sounds straightforward enough, as, indeed, does the justification of it repeatedly made on television and elsewhere by Government and EEC spokespersons. All that tedious and costly changing of money at the border crossing will be gone with the stroke of a pen. Who could possibly object to that? Is it not just plain common sense? Is it indeed not scandalous that business people and tourists should not have been able to benefit from it years ago?

Even cursory reflection on what a single currency will mean for national independence, and indeed what the Maastricht Treaty says it will mean, may put the matter into a rather different light. There is first the question of the nature of the institution that will be required to establish and to run a single currency. Maastricht is quite clear about this. It will be a single central bank, which will have the 'exclusive right to authorise the issue of bank notes in the Community'. The Bank shall not 'seek or take instructions from Community institutions or bodies, from any government of a member state or from any other body'. In other words, it will be completely independent and accountable to nobody. This is particularly significant since its Governing Council will have the power 'to decide upon the use of such other operational methods of monetary control as it sees fit, respecting Article 2'. Article 2 lays down its primary object as being to 'maintain price stability'.

To give away total and absolute control over the issue of its coinage and of all the ways of controlling credit is no mean step for a sovereign country to take. One does not need to enter the higher flights of economic fancy to be aware of the fact that he who controls the supply of money in all its facets controls most of the levers of economic management. If you are an economist of the pure monetarist school, you will believe that surrender of the monetary levers is to hand over all that matters in the conduct of economic policy.

You do not have to be a monetarist to imagine highly probable circumstances in which the loss of control of its currency by a nation state will lead naturally and swiftly to the handing over by it of other economic powers. A pan-European single currency will mean that countries with relatively high unit costs will no longer be able to devalue their currencies. Ultimately, under conditions of free trade, many of the industries and services of these unsuccessful countries will therefore go out of business and they will suffer rising unemployment. There will in these circumstances be seen to be a requirement for a compensatory shift in resources from the 'successful' countries to those which are, albeit perhaps temporarily, 'unsuccessful'. These compensatory expenditure decisions will of necessity need to be taken at the central, Federalist level. There will by this process have emerged a central fiscal policy which will need to be financed by centrally raised taxation. It was for this reason that I wrote in the *Guardian* in July 1991:

> A single currency means a single monetary authority, means a single government in everything that counts.

I returned to the point in a speech in Oxford on 12 June 1992:

> The right to raise taxes and to choose expenditure priorities is the very essence of national democratic sovereignty. It is what in this country civil wars have been fought over.

15

A move to a central currency is therefore something more than an operation to close down the money-changers. It is of itself about the most damaging single act that could be effected against a nation's ability to manage its own affairs. If it were to become genuinely 'irrevocable', it would be lethal to the continued existence of the nation as an independent entity.

The Treaty on European Union sets out to effect precisely this combination. There can be no doubt, therefore, of its monumental historic significance, whether or not it is enacted in the immediate future. The question remains whether the Maastricht route is the only one open to those who would bring about a State of Europe.

There is no doubt – Maastricht or no Maastricht – that the Treaty of Rome has spawned a set of institutions and instruments for economic management which have developed an apparently relentless momentum of their own. They are supported by a rapidly expanding legal system which increasingly claims supremacy over the laws of the nation states. Whether all this movement is now unstoppable and will inevitably reach the point where it will have become a matter of fact that national sovereignty has passed into other hands will be a central question which I shall try to answer as this book develops.

A substantial body of legal opinion – though as yet not the majority of lawyers – believes that the point of no return has already been passed, that Community law is now the ultimate source of authority in the land. This view I suspect is what prompted the former Lord Chief Justice, Lord Denning, to revise the famous imagery that he created of the Treaty of Rome as the 'incoming tide' flowing relentlessly into the estuaries and up the rivers, to this rather different appreciation of the situation:

No longer is European law an incoming tide flowing

up the estuaries of England. It is like a tidal wave bringing down the sea walls and flowing inland over our fields and houses . . . to the dismay of all.[1]

Nor is it just a matter of the relentless rush of law and precedent. In economic matters, too, many people argue that the die is now cast. The agreement reached between finance ministers on 27 July 1992 to hand over control of VAT to a central body has suggested to several commentators that the basis for a single taxing authority is with us already and that in this case Maastricht will simply formalise the *de facto* situation.

In the pages that follow I will put to the test Lord Denning's view that in effect 'the game is up', that a federal state exists already; I will consider another proposition, that until and unless we accept formally or *de facto* the principle of irrevocability, supreme authority remains in our hands: in the hands, that is, of those who elect people like me to Parliament.

I shall need also to analyse the views of those who agree that the process of federalisation in Europe is close to getting out of hand, but who are more fatalistic – they would no doubt call it pragmatic – about what can be done to change course.

The 'fatalists' fall into several well-defined groups and their various positions are worth briefly considering.

There are those first of all who argue that the whole process of attempting to kill off the nation state is so absurd that it will fall apart from the weight of its own stupidity. This view is broadly represented, for instance, by the well-respected 'Eurosceptical' columnist, Norman Macrae. Writing in the *Sunday Times* of 5 July 1992, he suggested: 'The Maastricht Treaty is meaningless nonsense so there is no

---

[1] Quoted by Martin Howe in *Europe and the Constitution after Maastricht*, published by the Society of Conservative Lawyers.

harm in ratifying it. It can better be killed by helpless laughter than getting cross.'

This is a variant of a view that is undoubtedly held by several British ministers and senior officials. They are able to suppress their profound misgivings about what they admit are serious concessions which have been made towards monolithic rule in Europe by arguing that 'since they will never work, there is no point in being seen to rock the boat by pointlessly withholding cooperation'. Cabinet ministers with direct responsibility for European matters have in the past expressed to me the view that much of what they agreed to was so 'ridiculous' that it would 'self-destruct'. This argument could presumably be pushed to the point of saying that the more outrageous the proposal, the more self-destructive its potential and therefore the greater the incentive to sign it.

Meanwhile, the Federalists are happy to join in the laughter. 'Never mind the jokes,' they say, 'just watch for the signature at the bottom of the Treaty. The Commission and the Court of Justice will do the rest, as they have done so successfully and with an increasing pace for the past thirty-five years.'

A second body of sceptical, not to say concerned, opinion which nevertheless argues for 'going along with the process' bases itself on an *à la carte* theory of European development. The suggestion is that the signatory can pick and choose its way through a menu of options, discarding the bits that do not suit its particular taste. As seen through British eyes, this has been the approach adopted by such countries as France, Italy, and the poorer nations. Informally it involves non-compliance with the rules. At a formal level it relies on 'Declarations' attached to treaties and on intergovernmental pronouncements and agreements such as that which took place in Luxembourg in 1966 at the insistence of General de Gaulle. Through the Luxembourg Accord, it was agreed that essential national interests

18

would always override Treaty commitments. The dubious legal standing of these exemptive arrangements will be discussed in some detail later. Suffice it to say for the present that so far as the increasingly powerful Court of Justice is concerned, what matters is what is in the main text of the Treaty.

Finally, there are those who argue that the European Community can be moulded 'from the inside'. By being ever ready to sign up to the further expansion of the scope, competence and power of its instruments, by being at the very 'centre' of the whole process, they argue that they can fashion and shape it into their own image and make it work for their purpose. Since this is the essence of currently professed British official policy in Europe, it is a point of view which merits examination in some depth. For that to be possible, it is necessary first to take a deeper look at the workings and the interactions of the main institutions of what, until and unless the Maastricht Treaty on European Union becomes the law of the land, we may still call the European Economic Community. Then we must ask what it is that Britain has been working for 'from within' and whether in so doing she has achieved her purpose. Not only will a closer inspection of the workings of the EEC hopefully throw some light on the soundness or otherwise of the British policy of 'arguing from within', it will also raise the crucial matter of what the centralist solution for Europe has to offer by way of democratic accountability. Can a Federalist state of Europe equip itself with a democratic system at least as effective as that provided by nationally elected Parliaments and executive bodies? This is a crucial matter. If the answer is in any doubt, then the case for the continued existence of the nation state re-exerts itself.

The crunch question, of course, will arise should we decide, for whatever reasons, that the nation state is worth preserving and that the British approach of 'changing from within' is failing in its purpose. We may then of necessity

19

have to ask the question: Is there an alternative to Britain's present policy of giving way step by step to not only economic but political union? It is often suggested – indeed, it is the federalists' fall-back position – that there is no alternative to the present course. If this were the case, those who have reservations about the direction that events are taking (ostensibly including the British Government) would have to accept that they had lost all power to bargain further. More important, we would then indeed have crossed the point of no return and would know with certainty that we were no longer citizens of a sovereign state.

Chapter 2

The Momentum of History

IT IS important to be clear from the outset what has been the nature of the historical development of the EEC and of Britain's involvement with it: How has the Community come to take on its present form? Was the goal of a federal union built in at its inception? To what extent do the historical experiences of Britain and her Continental neighbours merge? Is the force of present events irresistible?

Advocates of a federal Europe certainly claim a long pedigree for their vision. The names of Charlemagne and Charles V are in their mouths as are those of Bonaparte and Hitler on the lips of their opponents. The move towards integration as we know it today arose out of the Second World War. The impulse towards Federalism represented not so much a reasoned response to new circumstances caused by the war as a vague but passionate feeling that such things must be prevented from recurring. W. B. Curry, for example, who confessed to 'a conscious hatred of the sovereign state and all that it implies', published his *Case for Federal Union* in the early days of the war. Although in fact an argument for world rather than European Federation,

Curry's work is a good example of the essentially emotional anti-nationalism which was then gaining in strength; his arguments boil down to a sense that, since nation states fight each other, nation states must go.

Such feelings were becoming widespread in Western Europe during the mid-1940s. As early as 1943 René Massigli, de Gaulle's Foreign Policy Commissioner, began to look forward to 'an actual federation among France, Belgium, Luxembourg and Holland, which Great Britain might also join' (quoted from *New Europe*, a report for the French Resistance). The extent to which the emotional pacifism of the post-war years influenced the early development of the EEC can be seen in the text of the Treaty of Paris by which, on 18 April 1951, was established the European Coal and Steel Community. I quote the preamble of this in full to demonstrate how much more emphasis was put on European peace than on economic cooperation.

The President of the Federal Republic of Germany, His Royal Highness the Prince Royal of Belgium, the President of the French Republic, the President of the Italian Republic, Her Royal Highness the Grand Duchess of Luxembourg, Her Majesty the Queen of the Netherlands,

Considering that world peace can be safeguarded only by creative efforts commensurate with the dangers that threaten it.

Convinced that the contribution which an organised and vital Europe can make to civilisation is indispensable to the maintenance of peaceful relations.

Recognising that Europe can be built only through practical achievements which will first of all create real solidarity, and through the establishment of common bases for economic development.

Anxious to help, by expanding their basic production,

to raise the standard of living and further the works of peace.

Resolved to substitute for age-old rivalries the merging of their essential interest; to create, by establishing an economic community, the basis for a broader and deeper community among peoples long divided by bloody conflicts; and to lay the foundations for institutions which will give direction to a destiny henceforward shared.

Have decided to create a European Coal and Steel Community . . .

It is, of course, quite understandable that the peoples of Europe should have been deeply concerned with preventing another war among themselves. It is likewise easy to appreciate why, in the 1940s and 1950s, the pacifist ideal was closely linked with the idea of 'containing' nationalism in some form of supranational structure. In Continental Europe, nationalist thinking had become intertwined with Fascist and Nazi ideology. This was in complete contrast to Britain's wartime experience, where patriotism and the sense of nationhood had been the focus of resistance against Nazi totalitarianism.

It is worth considering for a moment the notion that nationalism is the chief cause of war, together with the often-asserted corollary that the European Economic Community is a force for peace. This way of thinking often surfaces amongst the generation which experienced the Second World War and was part of the surge of idealism that followed it.

While the belief that nationhood is the cause of war does somehow have a ring of plausibility, it has no real historical basis. Nationalism represents the drive of a people united by language, religion, culture or tradition to form an independent, unitary and self-governing state. Far from implying hostility to other nations, it was hailed by eighteenth- and early nineteenth-century political thinkers as the greatest force for democracy, peace and liberty in Europe. Historically, the greatest wars of the last two centuries have been motivated not by nationalism but by ideology: Jacobin, Bonapartist, Communist or National Socialist. In each one of these cases, nationalism has been distinguished by its record of resistance against totalitarianism. Where nationalism has been at the root of war, that conflict has invariably been provoked by the stubbornness and belligerence of a supranational state – be it Habsburg, Ottoman or, indeed, Yugoslav – in refusing to grant national self-government to its peoples.

If one of the motive forces present from the earliest days of the EEC was the idea that nations must federate for the sake of peace, the other was the influence of France. France enjoyed an unchallenged political supremacy in the Community from 1951 until 1973, when her hegemony was diluted by the Community's expansion, combined with the growing influence of Germany. Many French political concepts became woven into the fabric of the EEC during its early years. An analysis of French attitudes to Europe is indispensable to an understanding of the shape which the EEC had taken, and the direction in which it was moving, when Britain was allowed to join.

De Gaulle, whose personality dominated European as well as French politics at this time, held strongly to 'a certain idea of Europe', dominated by France and 'counter-balancing' the American and Soviet power blocs. Speaking in Algiers in May 1944, he proposed a 'kind of Western grouping' whose 'cornerstone' would be 'the most powerful and most numerous state of Europe', France, which would 'assume a European role for the benefit of everybody'.

Writing in his memoirs, de Gaulle made clear the geographical limitations which he intended for this European association. It would be firmly dominated by France, which should 'play a splendid role and greatly further her own interests and those of the human race'. France would sit 'in a position of authority in the old Continent, while America would find herself back in her hemisphere, and Britain in her island'.

By 1950, de Gaulle was speaking of 'the whole conception of Charlemagne', and France was preparing to assume the undisputed leadership of the EEC. The ideas for which de Gaulle is remembered – leading Europe to superpower status so as to 'resist' the Americans – are far too deeply ingrained into French political culture to be thought of simply as 'Gaullist'. The main poster employed by the French Socialist Government during the Maastricht referendum campaign portrayed grossly caricatured Americans and Japanese dominating the world and carried the slogan, 'Faire l'Europe c'est faire le poids' (To make Europe is to make a 'heavyweight').

To what extent do the ideological foundations upon which European union was constructed in the post-war era correspond to British national interests?

Take, first, the old Gaullist fear of Anglo-Saxon infiltration, which lives on today in the Commission's mistrust of American 'cultural imperialism' as enunciated by its Cultural Directorate DG-X (see *Culture Vultures*, by Adam Breeze, IFF, 1992). Britain's admission to the EEC required Prime Minister Edward Heath to assure President Pompidou that Britain was prepared to loosen her ties with what had hitherto been her chief ally. Anti-Americanism, although a sacred cow of French politicians from Left and Right alike, is also found elsewhere across Europe, most notably in the doctrine of the 'Third Way' or 'Special Path' which is part of the thinking of the German Social Democrat Party, the SPD. This anti-Americanism is clearly at cross-purposes with the interests of Britain's membership of Nato, arguably the strongest and most beneficial alliance into which the United Kingdom has ever entered.

25

Secondly, and closely related to the desire to be free from American influence, is the idea of Europe as a self-sufficient trading bloc competing with an American grouping in the West and a Japanese-led Pacific bloc in the East. It has to be said that the only two previous attempts to build such a trading system have not been auspicious. Napoleon's Continental System, which aimed to replace trade barriers within Europe by a single tariff around Europe, collapsed in disarray in 1814, having destroyed most of Europe's trading prosperity while ironically prompting a surge in British exports. The other plan, the 'Mitteleuropa' proposed by Walter Rathenau and other German businessmen in 1914, and revived during the Second World War as Albert Speer's 'Grossraumwirkschaft', was intended to lead to the de-industrialisation of Eastern and Southern Europe for the benefit of German industry. In neither case was Britain seen as part of the European trading bloc. With a permanent interest in world free trade and access to the open sea (or 'le grand large', as de Gaulle translated the phrase), Britain was recognised as being unlikely to wish to participate in a protectionist Europe.

The third element in the philosophical development of the EEC has been the idea of deploying Federalism to counter-balance what were seen to be the perversions of nationalism. The idea that the EEC would bring about a reconciliation between France and Germany was certainly a major objective of Robert Schuman, Jean Monnet and the others who played leading parts in the early process of European integration. The premiss, however, was rather ill-founded. Franco-German understanding during the post-war years owed more to the statesmanship of Adenauer and de Gaulle and to the changes wrought in the German polity by the experience of defeat in 1945, than it did to the formation of new pan-European institutions in Brussels. De Gaulle himself wrote of his relationship with the German leader, 'Adenauer agreed with me that there could be no question of submerging the identities of our two nations in a stateless institution' (quoted in Christopher Tugendhat's *Making Sense of Europe*, Viking, 1986).

What is equally clear is that the European Economic Community was (and still is) seen by most French politicians as the way to preserve and to legitimise the Franco-German ascendancy in Europe. The suggestion of some German commentators that the European ideal is more all-embracing than the Franco-German alliance has been specifically denounced by, for instance, the former French Foreign Minister, Jean-François Poncet, as 'a hypocritical way of trying to abandon the Europe of Jean Monnet' ('Quelle politique étrangère?' *Le Monde*, 9 October 1990).

All these strands of thought were clearly present in the European Economic Community from the moment of the formation of the European Coal and Steel Community. Britain joined the European Economic Community in 1972 in the belief that she could provide balance and modify what was already developing into a French-dominated (later Franco-German-dominated), anti-American, protectionist grouping with an institutional bias against unfettered national independence.

The question is how these ambitions on Britain's part to change the nature and direction of the EEC from within have worked out in practice. In particular, has the fact of British membership helped to restrain the movement towards political union, at least to the point where the choice remains open?

The Treaty of Rome, signed in March 1957, left open the issue of Federalism; it 'determined to lay the foundations for an ever-closer union among the people of Europe', and established EEC competence in the fields of transport, trade and agriculture. It also created an EEC role in social policy (Articles 117–122), this being seen as a 'balance' against the establishment of a free internal market. Far more important, however, the Treaty of Rome provided that Community

27

law, including the judgments of the European Court and the directives and regulations of the Commission, must be incorporated into the national laws of the Member States. It thus set into motion a process of self-powered and continuous centralisation.

In retrospect it should have been clear at least by the beginning of the 1960s that the embryo of a Federalist movement had taken life. The political situation at that time was not dissimilar to that of today: Walter Hallstein, the President of the Commission, who liked to be known as 'President of Europe', pursued the same supranational dreams as does his distant heir Jacques Delors. General de Gaulle's arguments would be familiar to any anti-Federalist today. His wish was for a 'Europe à l'anglaise', albeit 'sans les Anglais'.

The 1960s witnessed the decline of the Gaullist vision of a loose confederation under French leadership and the emergence of the Euro-nationalist philosophy. In July 1961, at the very moment when Harold Macmillan announced Britain's intention to seek membership of the EEC, Adenauer was presiding over a summit meeting of the Six in Bad Godesberg. The summit was considered the high point of the Gaullist campaign for an 'Europe des patries', and yet the final communiqué reveals how much had been conceded. It stated the resolve of the Six 'to give substance to the wish for political union already explicit in the treaties establishing the European Communities', and proposed to extend cooperation to the fields of education, culture and defence. Most important of all, the Treaty was to be revised after three years in the hope of further progress towards common policies. It is clear, therefore, that the Federalist 'ratchet effect', complementing the existing daily amassment of power by the EEC institutions, had commenced by the time of Britain's first application to join the Community.

The early years of the 1960s were significant also in demonstrating two other continuous strands in the development of the EEC: the widening rift between the political leaders and their unconsulted peoples; and the failure of attempts to promote a non-federal Europe by compromising with the EEC institutions as part of a process of 'arguing from within'.

The first two decades after the signing of the Treaty of Paris saw a balance being struck between French determination to unite Europe against American domination, and a desire elsewhere in Europe to establish a supranational majority voting structure for the union to avoid French domination. These diplomatic objectives were the undertakings of the political élites. Never was the issue of whether political control should be transferred to centralised European bodies conceived of as a matter for public debate in any of the countries concerned.

De Gaulle and his negotiators were prepared to surrender elements of sovereignty as the price for uniting Europe behind France to raise France's standing and prestige. The smaller countries' diplomats, fearful of French or Franco-German hegemony, at first sought to balance France by procuring Britain's admission to the EEC. When it became clear that the British application would be vetoed, their alternative was to contain France within a centralised federal structure. Federalism was thus born from the union between de Gaulle's will to integrate Europe for the benefit of France, and the converse aim of the Dutch Foreign Minister, Joseph Luns, and his Belgian counterpart, Paul-Henri Spaak, to ensure that any union which emerged was properly supranational. Never were the French, Dutch or Belgian electorates directly consulted about all this. De Gaulle's proposal in 1960 that there should be a Europe-wide referendum on political union went disregarded by each government.

On the occasions when referendums have been held on European union, the politicians have invariably lined up as one to press the case for integration. The recent referendums in Denmark, Ireland and France all displayed the common theme of a united political establishment – politicians of every main party, television, newspapers, business – throwing its weight behind the ratification of Maastricht. In each of these, television and/or radio broadcasts were sequestered by the Government (there were four 'vote yes' broadcasts in Ireland to one 'vote no'); public money was used to promote a 'yes' vote, and spending on the 'yes' campaign massively outweighed that on the 'no'. In Denmark several businesses actually threatened to move abroad if the Treaty did not receive public backing. If public opinion had reflected opinion in Parliament or levels of funding during the campaigns, opposition to Maastricht would have been unlikely to reach 10 per cent in any of these referendums.

The practice of surrendering sovereignty, with no mandate, as part of domestic horse-trading has become general in Europe. The transformation of the European Assembly into an elected Parliament, for example, was accepted by Britain as part of the price paid by the Callaghan Government for Liberal support. This process is all the more significant when one bears in mind the second common theme of European integration: the inability of the opponents of Federalism to advance their case by arguing 'from the heart of Europe'. For it is clear that any sacrifices of sovereignty made to this end are made in vain.

In France during the early years of the Fifth Republic, in pursuit of a non-federal Europe, de Gaulle began by employing the 'heart of Europe' strategy, which ended in disaster when his colleagues demanded that he live up to his rhetoric. He then switched to what might be termed a 'No, no, no' strategy, and inflicted on the central institutions of the EEC the only real set-back which they have suffered in their otherwise steady amassment of power.

In the early 1960s, de Gaulle's Government pursued a policy of speaking the language of a 'good European', of entering headlong into negotiations over European union, of always appearing 'positive', while at the same time quietly working from within for a loose grouping of co-operative states. The result of this policy was the alienation of the Federalists, who accepted de Gaulle's concessions and continued undeflected on the course of supranationality. France had achieved nothing: her model of Europe was no closer to being adopted, and she was now isolated from the other five states.

In 1965, faced with Commission proposals massively to increase the budget and to transfer powers from the Council to the Assembly, de Gaulle changed tack. France walked out of the Council and, on 7 July, announced that she would boycott the European Communities until further notice. By the end of the year, this policy of honesty and consistency had borne fruit: the Commission climbed down from its proposals and France rejoined the EEC on the basis of the Luxembourg compromise.

While most of the concessions to de Gaulle have since been eroded, the French action of 1965 ranks with the result of the Danish referendum of 1992 as one of only two occasions when the inexorable advance of Federalism has been temporarily checked.

What of Britain's involvement with the EEC?

A brief reflection on Britain's record in Europe at the time when the EEC was formed reveals the hollowness of the assertion that Britain has been insular or anti-European in her outlook. Having played a critical role in the liberation of Europe in 1944, Britain helped to lead the way in the creation and the maintenance of Nato; she made a heavy investment of men and resources in the defence of Europe through the British Army of the Rhine. Active in seeking to rebuild Europe after the ravages of war, Britain reimposed rationing at home to help the starving people of Germany, and even gave Germany 25 per cent of her Marshall Aid. (Some of this is still part of a capital fund making cheap loans available to Germany industry.) So far from being 'Little England', Britain was a vigorous supporter of the Council of Europe and worked strenuously for the establishment of free trade through the sixteen-member Organisation for European Economic Cooperation.

Her internationalism, however, was matched by an opposition to supranationalism. The wartime experience of the United Kingdom had been profoundly different from that of Continental countries. In consequence, the British people did not share in the widespread distaste in Europe for nationalism, nor in the belief that nation states had become outdated. Rather, they continued to trust and to cherish their legal and governmental institutions, which – alone in Europe – had led them to prevail over the dictatorships. Across Europe, nationalism had been corrupted by racism, collaboration and tyranny. In Britain it had stood for the defence of liberty against Nazism. Moreover, neither the British Government nor the British people saw their destiny as wholly and exclusively European. Britain had special interests across the world which would be threatened by her submersion into a West European Federation. Her overseas trade would clearly suffer as the result of protectionist tariffs around Europe, and her relationship with the United States would be damaged by the anti-Americanism which lurked behind much of the European supranationalist rhetoric.

The integrationist governments of Western Europe, while welcoming Britain's goodwill and her contributions to the economic regeneration and defence of Europe, had their own, very different, objectives. The contrast between a British vision of an open and free Europe, and the Continental perspective of a protectionist, subsidy-based, politically united Europe guarding its interests against the rest of the world, was thus present from the earliest years of the EEC.

Although unwilling to allow Britain to become part of a

federal state, British Conservative Governments after 1951 worked hard to build a wide Europe of tariff-free and closely cooperating nation states. Britain's failure to participate in the Messina Conference of 1955, so often condemned as the root of British difficulties with the EEC, is quite explicable. Since the Governments of the Six were set upon the course of building a protectionist customs union based upon agricultural subsidies and with the distant goal of Federation, Britain found herself in a very difficult position. She dispatched an observer to argue the case for a wide, free-trade zone based on the OEEC; the arguments fell on deaf ears. In 1956, Britain formally proposed a European Free Trade Association (Efta) based on the OEEC and excluding agricultural and Commonwealth trade – the so-called Plan G. The British position was wholly incompatible with that of the Six, and served only to spur them on to greater haste in negotiating the Treaty of Rome.

In direct response, in May 1960 the United Kingdom formed the seven-member Efta, a tariff-free area which neither limited trade with third countries nor aimed for an 'ever closer union' among its peoples. The member states were Austria, Britain, Denmark, Norway, Portugal, Sweden and Switzerland.

In July 1961, having announced Britain's intention to seek membership of the EEC for herself and the Efta countries, Harold Macmillan dispatched a negotiating team, headed by Edward Heath, to discover on what terms they might be accepted. In August 1961, Edward Heath explained Britain's negotiating position to a preliminary plenum in Paris. He asked for some reduction in the common external tariffs, exemption for elements of Commonwealth trade, British autonomy in agriculture and full or associate membership for the Efta Seven. These terms were wholly unacceptable to the EEC. The view of the Six was that the growth of the Community into a united and self-contained superpower could never survive such an expansion, nor such an open attitude to trade with the rest of the world.

The external tariffs of the EEC and the Common Agricultural Policy (CAP) have always been largely politically rather than economically motivated. There is certainly little economic justification in compelling the European consumer to pay inflated prices for food while simultaneously paying heavy taxes to increase food production (much of which is then destroyed), crippling the economies of the Third World in the process. If Britain were to be allowed to join the European Economic Community, however, she would have to accept the CAP and the external tariffs (both of which would damage her, a food importer with much overseas trade, far more than any of the Six) as a sign of her political commitment to the European ideal.

Britain's position in 1962 and 1963 was the same as it had been in 1955: she would not join a protectionist, anti-American bloc with (at least since 1961) a clear programme of developing common policies. Her application was formally vetoed by de Gaulle in 1963.

The incompatibility of the British view of Europe and that of the governments of the Six was again demonstrated four years later when Harold Wilson made Britain's second application for membership. Wilson announced that Britain would join 'provided the terms were right', and then spelt out those terms, emphasising the importance of independence in defence and foreign affairs and of the right to buy cheap food. This was no more acceptable to the Euronationalist governments than had been Britain's previous offer, and her application was once again vetoed. It was by now clear that British membership of the EEC would be contingent upon her willingness to accept both the economic costs of the agricultural and trade policies and the political costs of alienating many of her non-European friends and partners, as well as of her acceptance of the principle of ever-closer Federation.

The British electorate had by this time become aware of

this. At the beginning of the 1970s, opinion polls were running at three or four to one against joining the EEC; many of the candidates in the 1970 election had undertaken – in response to a Voters' Veto Campaign – to oppose British entry into the EEC on any terms. Edward Heath, the Conservative Party leader, had pledged 'to negotiate; no less, no more', and added that Britain would join the EEC only 'with the full-hearted consent of Parliament and people'.

In 1972 Britain in effect dropped the objections which she had held for the previous twenty years and accepted the imposition of EEC trade and agriculture policies in full, negotiating a short transition period for their implement-ation. Her prime minister assured the French President that he was prepared to reassess Britain's worldwide role in the light of her 'new' commitment to Europe and accepted the principle of full political cooperation. For the next ten years, until Margaret Thatcher negotiated a rebate at the Fontaine-bleau summit, the British contribution to the EEC budget was disproportionately swollen, while Britain went from an overall trade surplus in manufactured goods with the countries of the Six of £385 million in 1970 (effectively the last pre-entry year) to a deficit with the EEC of £3,410 million in 1979.

It is reasonable to suppose that Britain could have joined the EEC on such terms at any time. The suggestion that Britain could have arrested the development of supranation-alism, protectionism and subsidy had she become a member of the EEC earlier than she did is somewhat questionable. Britain was not allowed to join *precisely because* she would not agree to the specific and stringent terms which she was offered.

In 1972, the European Communities Act passed through Parliament with a majority of eight. In 1974, on an implicitly anti-EEC manifesto, Harold Wilson was returned to office in two general elections. Since then, no major party has offered the British electorate at a general election the option of expressing dissatisfaction with the development of the EEC. Although the Labour manifesto of 1983 suggested withdrawal, this pledge – like the perennial Labour commitment to abolish the House of Lords – was not widely seen as likely to be put into practice. In the absence of an electoral option, the 1975 Referendum constituted the only occasion when the British people were able to express an opinion on the European Economic Community. In considering the question of precisely what sort of a mandate this was, it is worth remembering the circumstances in which the vote was taken.

The Conservative Party was campaigning on its record of having taken Britain into the EEC three years previously. The promises made by the Government in those days were unambiguous: 'There is no question of any erosion of essential national sovereignty . . .' The Labour Government was equally unequivocal in its assurances. Its official pamphlet in 1975 stated: 'No important new policy can be decided in Brussels without the consent of a British Minister answerable to a British Government and British Parliament.'

So, far from acquiring a mandate for European integration in 1975, the Government was able to gain consent for continued membership of the EEC only on the basis of a specific and explicit promise that British sovereignty was in no way threatened.

The British people have never consented to any diminution of their right to be governed by laws and men and women of their own choosing. Nor, indeed, have they ever been given the opportunity to express a collective opinion on the subject. The process towards Federalisation has continued above the heads of the people, who still essentially conceive of the whole European adventure as one of strengthening the bonds of friendship and cooperation with neighbouring countries. The idea of switching allegiance to a new political entity has only very recently begun to cross their minds and it has provoked the outright hostility of the majority.

British Governments, having accepted the terms of entry into the EEC, have concentrated their efforts on trying to mould its institutions and policies to suit the open-trading and non-Federalist perspectives of the people. Let us see how successful they have been.

Chapter 3

'Compromising from Within': The Institutions

FROM THE start of her membership of the EEC – and, indeed, well before – Britain has had her doubts about the direction in which Europe was going. At the moment of joining, she was able to suppress these anxieties on the basis of a belief that, once inside, she would be able to use her diplomatic skills to change things in her own image.

Despite each rebuff, each 'compromise' which was in reality a concession, each lost argument in the Council of Ministers, Britain has persisted with the idea that she could argue her fellow Members into a change of course. The style may have changed with the switch in premiership from Margaret Thatcher to John Major: there is now talk of a 'positive approach' and of 'being at the heart of Europe'.

Ostensibly, however, the policy remains the same: the rhetoric of the British Government continues to be anti-Federalist. If there has been a substantive change towards a genuinely more Federalist position, it will have to be left to future historians to discover. For the present, one must take it as one finds it. Certainly, on the face of it, the British position remains one of arguing for a non-federal, free-trading, closely associating group of independent nation states. Its method of doing so is to 'argue from within' and then to accept whatever emerges.

The question is whether, despite the set-backs, this is a sensible approach for Britain to pursue. Later it may be necessary to ask whether it is the only approach open to her.

There are two ways in which it may be possible for Britain successfully to alter the shape of the EEC from within. The first is for her to modify the nature of the institutions of the EEC; the second is to achieve a change in the general direction of policy.

What is the probability that Britain will be able to re-fashion the new institutions of Europe? There are, in fact, three European Communities: the European Coal and Steel Community (ECSC), established by the Treaty of Paris in 1951; the European Economic Community (EEC), which under the terms of the Maastricht Treaty is to be known simply as the European Community (EC); and the European Atomic Energy Community (Euratom), which, along with the EEC, was established by the Treaty of Rome in 1957.

The three Communities are served by four common institutions: the European Parliament, the Court of Justice, the Council and the Commission. The latter two of these institutions only became common to the three Communities in 1967: the merger was intended as the first step towards creating a single European Community to be governed under a single Treaty – a scheme which has not since been pursued. The Maastricht Treaty will set up a fifth institution, the European Central Bank.

THE COMMISSION

The Commission has seventeen members, with each Community country providing either one or two (Treaty on European Union (Maastricht Treaty), Article 157). Their term of office is five years and renewable (ibid., Article 158(1)). While the European Parliament has the theoretical right to dismiss the Commission *en masse*, there is absolutely no mechanism for censuring individual Commissioners, and the Parliament's supposed right is likely to remain unused. Commissioners, once ensconced in office, are accountable to no one, just as they were elected by no one.

The President of the Commission and his six Vice-Presidents are appointed by 'common accord' (Article 158(2)) among the Governments of the Member States. While this might seem to give a veto to national governments, no such power operates in practice. The most recent appointment of the Commission's President, that of Jacques Delors at the Lisbon Summit in June 1992, is an example of the effective majority rule which prevails on these occasions. The British Conservative Government had made no secret of its objection to M. Delors' vision of Europe: 'In my view', said John Major in 1992, 'the Delors route is quite the wrong way for the future development of Europe.' Yet, with the other eleven Member States agreed on his reappointment, Britain was hardly in a position to secure his post for a candidate of her own. Delors' political beliefs were no secret: he had, as the French Finance Minister, pursued a brand of interventionist socialism which had so retarded and crippled the French economy that President Mitterrand had proposed his Brussels appointment in order to be rid of him (see Russell Lewis, 'Master Eurocrat – The Making of Jacques Delors'). Delors blamed the failure of his policies upon the fact that they could not succeed in one country in isolation,

40

and proposed to apply them on a European scale. The ambiguity of the phrase 'common agreement' and the practical impossibility of one or two countries prevailing against a consensus ensured his reappointment in 1992.

M. Delors' case illustrates the difficulty that a national government has in arresting the development of a particular ideology at the centre of the Community. If a majority of European governments is committed to placing a declared Federalist at the head of the Community's executive arm, the minority can do nothing but grind their teeth and abide by his directives.

The Commission departments are situated in Brussels and Luxembourg. Staff number a little over 14,000, of whom some three-quarters are from the original six nations of the European Community; over half the employees are provided by France, Belgium and Italy (see *The European Commission and the Administration of the Community*, Office for Official Publications of the European Communities, L-2985 Luxembourg). There is no longer any pretence that the Commission is merely a bureaucratic body staffed by civil servants. The members of the Commission are themselves all politicians who make no secret of their belief that they hold their positions in order to speed the progress of European integration. As long ago as 1970, the President of the Commission told the European Parliament: 'The Commission is, at one and the same time, the guardian of the Treaties and the motive force of integration' (quoted in Martin Howe, *Europe and the Constitution after Maastricht*, Society of Conservative Lawyers, June 1992).

Bearing in mind the urgent desire to build a centralised unitary European state which prevails in the Commission, it is worth noting its substantial powers for initiating legislation; these complement its executive powers.

The primary role of the Commission is that of 'guardian of the Treaties'. It has the power to investigate any alleged infringement of the Treaties or of the decisions of a

41

European institution; it may act on the strength of complaints from governments or individuals, or simply on its own initiative. The Commission may then instruct a Member State to alter any disputed practice, and refer the matter to the Court if it is not satisfied with the alteration. Acting in its executive capacity, the Commission issues dozens of regulations every day to force national governments to amend their policies; it also has the sole and arbitrary power to issue 'derogations' to particular Member States wishing to bypass the rules laid down in the Treaties. The danger of these arrangements arises out of the fact that the Commission has never seen itself merely as an impartial arbitrator holding the balance between the national interests of Member States; on the contrary, it consistently uses the powers it has to entrench the authority of the nascent European State which it seeks to create.

The second principal task performed by the Commission is that of administering the Community budget. Nearly two-thirds of this is consumed by the Common Agricultural Policy. Ever-increasing amounts of money are spent on straightforward geographical reallocation of wealth, 'Cohesion' as it is termed. The EEC budget has doubled since 1987, and now stands at £42,000 million.

The third, and most significant, function performed by the Commission is that of initiating Community policy. The power to formulate and to propose legislation gives the Commission a blank cheque to build and extend the powers of the embryonic European Government in wholly new forms and directions, with no control exercised by national Governments. A former Secretary-General of the Commission, writing in an official EEC publication in 1988, explained the position admirably:

Everything to do with economic union was left blank in the Treaty, but the blanks can be filled by the institutions. There is no need for fresh treaties or fresh parliamentary ratification. (Émile Noël, Office for Official Publications of the European Communities, L-2985 Luxembourg)

Thus, the phrase 'conveyor belt to Federalism' is one which would be cheerfully recognised in the Berlaymont building in Brussels. The Commission is not only given the authority to hasten moves to integration between and outside intergovernmental agreements, but defines its success in terms of doing so.

Among the new rights given to the Commission by the Maastricht Treaty is that of coercing Member States to adjust their economic policies with the aim of ensuring economic convergence, so as to establish a single currency with minimum delay. The Commission would be able to recommend to the Council that a Member State should rectify any Government deficit which the Commission deemed excessive. The Council could then, under Article 104(b), acting by a qualified majority and only on a recommendation from the Commission, fine any Member State which failed to comply with its recommendations.

Nobody any longer seriously seeks to deny that the unelected Commission has extraordinary powers to shape the direction of European policy, or that it is motivated by a mission to further the cause of European integration; and yet, under present arrangements, there is little that Britain or any other nation can do to check or delay, let alone to fetter, the processes by which the Commission continues to amass new areas of authority to itself every day.

THE COUNCIL

The Council is made up of representatives from the twelve Member States. The chief delegate of each country is its foreign minister, but the Council comprises different groups of ministers according to its purpose: agricultural, transport, industry, finance and so on. The Presidency of the Council is held for six months by each of the Member States in turn. The holders of this position in 1993 are Denmark and then Belgium, which will be followed by Greece, Germany, France, Spain and Italy. Tenure of the Presidency enables a country to influence the Community's agenda for six months, although it must act in consultation with the Commission. All meetings are chaired by the relevant minister from the state holding the Presidency, while a junior minister represents that state's particular interests. The Commission recently formulated proposals to abolish this system of rotation, and to put in its place a powerful and centralised executive Presidency of Europe (with the prime candidate to fill that office presumably being M. Delors).

The Council moves to a decision by a simple majority except where there are provisions to the contrary in the Treaties. These provisions may prescribe either unanimity or a qualified majority vote. In the case of the latter, a decision must receive 54 votes out of the total of 76. The votes of the Member States are weighted as follows: France, Germany, Italy and the United Kingdom each has ten votes (although Germany is demanding an increase following unification); Spain has eight votes; Belgium, Greece, the Netherlands and Portugal each has five; Denmark and Ireland each has three; and Luxembourg has two votes.

The Council has a staff in Brussels, the General Secretariat, of a little over 2,000 officials. In April, June and October, the Council holds its meetings in Luxembourg, while the other meetings are normally held in Brussels.

The most significant trend in the development of the Council is the continuing extension of majority voting and the consequent erosion of the power of veto by a nation state. The origins of this process lie in the early 1960s when, as now, there was a fierce debate as to whether Europe should follow the path of federal unification or that of intergovernmental cooperation, the 'Europe des patries' favoured by de Gaulle. The dispute culminated in the 'Luxembourg Compromise' of 1965, which was in reality no compromise at all, rather the maintenance of hostile stand-off. (The United Kingdom has only once formally invoked the 'Luxembourg Compromise', on 18 May 1982, during the agricultural price-fixing negotiations. It was overruled by the other members.) The years since 1965 have represented a gradual defeat of the Gaullist vision and of the principle of unanimity. Majority voting has now been extended to most areas central to European policy, including agriculture, transport, research and development and economic and social Cohesion.

The extent to which the Commission and the enthusiasts for Federalism in other national governments will seek to circumscribe what remains of unanimity should not be underestimated. One former Secretary-General of the Commission, writing after nearly thirty years of experience with Commission–Council negotiations, judged that 'even where unanimity is the rule, no member of the Community can disregard the general interest in assessing his own: unanimity in a Community cannot be equated with an absolute right of veto' (Émile Noël, op. cit.).

An example of this calculated emasculation of the veto exists in the 'Declaration on Voting in the Field of the Common Foreign and Security Policy' which comprises part of the Maastricht Treaty. This reads:

> The Conference agrees that, with regard to Council decisions requiring unanimity, Member States will, to the extent possible, avoid preventing a unanimous decision where a qualified majority exists in favour of that decision.

45

A recently developed technique by which the Commission and its supporters extend the areas covered by majority voting is simply to define any proposal which might not receive unanimous support as a 'Single Market' or as a 'health and safety' initiative. The Single European Act inserted two important provisions into the Treaty of Rome: Article 100A which deals with Single Market measures; and Article 188A which covers health and safety at work. Both provide for regulations and directives to be adopted under them by a qualified majority vote in the Council.

These Articles now comprise the means by which the Commission can sidestep the power of veto of Member States. For example, Britain's 'opt-out' of the Social Chapter of the Maastricht Treaty has proved to be less than fool-proof. When the Commission wishes to impose the constraints of the Social Chapter upon Britain, it merely defines those constraints as a 'health and safety' directive and applies them without needing the consent of the British Government. Thus, the 48-hour working week which was agreed to by the other eleven states under the terms of the Social Chapter was redefined as a 'health and safety' directive and imposed upon Britain under Article 118A. While the Government succeeded in gaining some exceptions and limitations, the principle that the EEC should regulate British employment policy has been conceded in perpetuity.

The power enjoyed by the Commission vis-à-vis the Council should never be underestimated. It is the Commission which draws up the proposal the Council is to discuss; only on the basis of that proposal can the Council deliberate at all. While the inadequacy of the current system, which places the initiative for moulding Europe in the hands of the Commission, is now widely recognised outside the Commission itself, it is important to stress that there are no moves towards strengthening the Council at the expense of the Commission. Those who propose to fill the 'democratic deficit' within the European Economic Community are not speaking of strengthening the Council, which represents the democratically elected governments of the Member States; on the contrary, they propose to weaken this body, which they see as insufficiently 'European' in its outlook, and to transfer its powers to the European Parliament. (The European Parliament has argued since 1984 that the process by which powers formerly exercised by national parliaments pass to the 'unelected' Council of Ministers must be eliminated. See David Millar (Europa Institute, University of Edinburgh) in *Parliamentary Brief*, July 1992.)

THE EUROPEAN PARLIAMENT

The European Parliament, formerly the European Assembly, consists of 518 MEPs, who meet for a week in every month at Strasbourg. While elected on a national basis, the MEPs sit in transnational political groups.

The MEPs have been directly elected since June 1979. While this development was not accompanied by any change in the powers of the Parliament, it conferred a certain apparent legitimacy upon it and opened a new front in the battle for European integration. Until 1979, the role of the Parliament was analogous to that of a shareholders' committee, scrutinising the worst excesses of the Commission. Its powers, then as now, were limited to the right to put questions to the Commission, to be consulted by the Commission, and the right to reject elements of the Community budget.

The Parliament also has the right to veto the accession of new states to the EC. Recently the Parliament has developed more substantial ambitions. Based upon the fact of the direct election of its members, the European Parliament

47

now seeks to have powers more suited to its self-defined role as the legislature of a new national state.

It is very difficult to see how parliamentary democracy could function effectively on a European scale. An electorate of 340 million, speaking twelve main languages and countless dialects, and accustomed to a myriad of differing political traditions, seems an unlikely recipe for democratic and accountable government. The essence of a democratic state is that each of its citizens feels sufficient community of interest with his or her fellow-electors to abide by their majority decisions and keep the laws made by their representatives, even if he or she personally did not cast his or her vote for those representatives. It is a very different matter when laws are imposed upon a country from abroad by an authority to which the citizens have no sense of allegiance and with which they do not identify.

Behind the rhetoric of 'filling the democratic deficit' and 'bringing Europe closer to the citizen' lie the hard facts which betray the hollowness of these phrases as well as the hostility to the nation state felt by many of their advocates. While Europe is essentially directed by the unelected and unaccountable Commission, the would-be democrats in the European Parliament devote their energies to gaining powers from the Council, which is the one body in the EEC having any role in upholding the national interests of the Member States and of their genuinely democratically accountable governments.

Nowhere is the will to establish a European national state more clearly visible than in the proposals to give the European Parliament the role, the status and all the trappings of a national parliament. Attempts to present this process as democratic are ill-founded. Public interest in the Strasbourg Parliament is slight. For such a body to be given powers hitherto exercised by national parliaments in order to build a centralised European superpower without the loyalty of its inhabitants would be a diminution of democracy and not an increase in it.

THE EUROPEAN COURT

The European Court of Justice is the supreme interpreter of Community law; any doubts over the function of Community law are referred to the European Court under Article 177 of the Treaty of Rome. The pronouncements of the Court are final and binding. It is thus extremely important to assess its powers and its motivation, and to form a view as to the impartiality it brings to its task.

The Court is located in Luxembourg. It consists of thirteen judges assisted by six Advocates-General. A Court of First Instance was attached to it in 1988, consisting of twelve members. Each judge is appointed for a term of office of six years, which may be renewed. Judgments are made by a secret and simple majority vote; there is no way of ascertaining whether any judges dissented from a judgment, and the deliberations of the judges are never publicly revealed.

The Anglo-Saxon tradition, based upon the concept of an inflexible rule of law, is occasionally at odds with the Continental tradition where the law, if inconvenient, can be set aside or altered for the political benefit of the state. The idea that written law must not be allowed to stand in the way of political necessity is one with a long pedigree in Continental Europe, and is central to the thinking of the European Court.

There is no doubt that the European Court has advanced its powers beyond those of a judiciary and has adopted a policy-making legislative function (see Gavin Smith, *The European Court of Justice: Judges or Policymakers?*). This development is illustrated by a series of judgments on the subject of equal pay. In *Defrenne* v. *Sabena* (1976) (see Howe, op. cit., p. 18), the European Court decided that the principle that men and women should receive equal pay for equal work, as outlined in Article 119 of the Treaty of Rome, should *from that moment* be directly applicable as part of the law of the Member States; the Court stated that the judgment could not be relied upon 'in order to support claims concerning pay periods prior to this judgment, except as regards those workers who have already brought legal proceeding or made an equivalent claim'. In 1990, in *Barber* v. *Guardian Royal Exchange*, the Court widened the definition of 'pay' to include redundancy terms and pension payments; again, their judgment was effective *only from that date* (ibid., p. 20). These judgments were manifestly legislative and not judicial acts; had they represented an interpretation of the law, they would not have been accompanied by declarations that they might take only prospective effect.

Given the Court's adoption of a policy-making role, and given that there is no possibility of appealing to a higher authority, its impartiality becomes of critical importance. The record of the Court and its own pronouncements combine to show it, however, as an avowed and vigorous force for centralisation (see H. Schermers, *The European Court of Justice: Promoter of Integration*, 1974). As early as 1960, in the *Netherlands* v. *High Authority* case, the power of the Court to rule on complaints against Member States was described as 'the *ultima ratio* enabling the Community interests enshrined in the Treaty to prevail over the inertia and resistance of Member States' (Howe, op. cit., p. 44).

The most common technique by which the European Court extends the scope of Community law is to seize upon the general principles outlined in the Treaties and to use these as the means by which to interpret any ambiguity within the law in a centralising direction. Thus has the Court cited Article 30 of the Treaty of Rome which prohibits restrictions on trade between Member States as justification for its interest in Britain's Sunday trading laws. As it happens, the Advocate-General advised that these laws should be left unchanged in order to 'accord with national socio-cultural characteristics', but the principle of EEC jurisdiction has been conceded. Similarly, Article 8A of the Single European Act, which guarantees the free movement of goods, persons, services and capital, is used as the basis of the EEC's challenge to the United Kingdom's attempt to retain her border controls.

This tendency of the Court to latch on to general principles is of very great significance when one considers the principles conceded in the Maastricht Treaty, and the fact that the European Court is to be responsible for their interpretation. British diplomats may to their own satisfaction have conceded some of that Treaty's clauses to be meaningless rhetoric, but it is quite clear from the record of the European Court that it employs them as a means of extending its jurisdiction.

The history of the European Court has been that of the continuing expansion of its powers. There is no method of appeal against this process, nor are there means of reversing the extension of EEC law into new areas. Under current institutional arrangements, the growth of this new Leviathan cannot be resisted.

EUROPEAN CENTRAL BANK

Articles 105 to 109 of the Maastricht Treaty provide for the establishment of a European Central Bank. This bank will be responsible for the monetary policy of the EEC, controlling the foreign reserves of the Member States and setting the exchange rate of the ECU against other currencies. It will also represent the EEC in international monetary institutions, although national central banks may also participate, subject to its approval.

The Central Bank arguably is the EEC institution most

likely to consummate the development of a politically
united Community. Control over monetary policy is central
to the function of government. Just as the transfer of power
from Crown to Parliament in England was born essentially
out of parliamentary control of economic policy, so is the
transfer of monetary policy from national Governments to a
European body intended to herald a fundamental shift in
political power.

The Central Bank is to be administered by an Executive
Board whose members are appointed for a period of eight
years by 'common accord' among the Governments of the
Member States. The weakness and ambiguity of the phrase
'common accord' has already been discussed. The deliberations of the Executive Board may not be made public. In
common with the Commission and the Court, the Central
Bank is thus to be unelected, unaccountable and secretive.
Its creation at this time must call into question any idea that
the drive towards undemocratic centralisation within the
EEC can be slowed or halted.

The British 'opt-out' from the Single Currency exempts
the United Kingdom from several elements of the Central
Bank's authority. What this arrangement is likely to mean
in practice will be discussed in Chapter 5.

The amount of power now held by the central institutions of the European Community, and the balance
between those institutions, must be disturbing to anyone
who supports open and accountable government. At present, the Commission is the real driving-force of the Community, exercising an increasingly frequently used power
to initiate legislation, and attracting new powers to itself by
the day. The Council, on the other hand, supposedly the
guardian of national as opposed to Community interests,
has been enfeebled in this role by the abolition – either by
treaty or through the Commission's power to sidestep it –
of the power of veto. The Court, intended as an impartial
referee, employs policy-making powers in order to further

the cause of European integration, and the proposed establishment of the European Central Bank demonstrates how great has been the acceleration in the process by which powers are being reallocated from national Governments to unelected central institutions. The European Parliament remains essentially powerless; to the extent of holding the Commission genuinely accountable, it is likely to remain so, despite its considerable ambitions to increase its powers.

The establishment of EEC 'competence' in a new area invariably requires no fresh treaty, no specially convened intergovernmental conference, no unanimity among Member States. The departure of the EEC into fresh areas, as seen in the Single European Act and in the Maastricht Treaty – into transport, research and development, social policy – was in each case a recognition of existing EEC competence in an area. The formal acknowledgment of the European Council and of European political cooperation in the Single European Act is an example of this process, as is the gradual EEC encroachment into the field of foreign policy.

There is, throughout, a tendency towards centralisation which has a momentum of its own. Operating the 'occupied field' theory, under which EEC authority is irremovably entrenched in any area in which it has once been used, the Commission and the Court continue to expand Community authority in what can only be conceived as a process of moving towards a United Europe. Since there is no way of controlling these institutions, nor any higher appeal body against the European Court of Justice, it is difficult to avoid the conclusion that under the current institutional arrangements, Europe is moving inexorably towards forming itself into a superstate.

There is no evidence to suggest that calls for reform have in any way slowed down the autocratic centralism of the EEC institutions, nor that the Court will ever reverse its policy of interpreting every law and every clause in the

Treaties as steps towards political union.

The only official proposals made for reform have been those of the European Parliament. These proposals, if adopted, would assist the process of centralisation, since they aim to remove further powers from national parliaments and from the Council, leaving untouched and unaccountable the Commission, the Court and the Central Bank. Even if a workable plan could be formulated to turn the Strasbourg Parliament into a replica of a national parliament for a united Europe, such elevation of the European Parliament would mean the irrevocable end of the United Kingdom as a self-governing democracy. British MEPs sit in a permanent minority in Strasbourg, and the will of their constituents would be overruled whenever a majority was raised against them. For such a system to function, the people of this country would have to see themselves primarily as Europeans, and therefore willing to abide by decisions made by French, Dutch and Greek voters with which they disagreed.

The speed of the momentum at which the EEC institutions are expanding their power is making the process virtually unstoppable. Certainly 'arguing from within' has done nothing to change the direction of events. The pace has merely quickened.

Consider the record of Britain's relations with the EEC over the past two years. In that time, Britain's political leaders have signed the Maastricht Treaty, conceding European citizenship, a European foreign policy, and the formal recognition of the entity which is to become the new state, the European Union. Britain has voted to reappoint Jacques Delors, whose Federalist intentions for Europe are well established. She has accepted that the EEC institutions may regulate how long her citizens work. And she has conceded in principle that the EEC may decide the rate of her indirect taxation. All these concessions have been made against the background of a matchless record of implementing the

Commission's directives and regulations. What has Britain gained in return?

The truth is that there have been no concessions of principle won by Britain. There are no examples of a British agenda being adopted by the EEC institutions.

The Maastricht Treaty, in particular, is both a demonstration of the continuing centralisation of the EEC and a consolidation of that process. From Britain's point of view, arguing the case for changing the institutions of the EEC 'from within' has not worked. Have there been other avenues open to her where she has been more successful in implanting her viewpoint on the EEC?

Chapter 4

'Compromising from Within': The Policies

IT IS arguable that successive British Governments, although paying lip service from time to time to the notion of being able to change the institutions of the EEC 'from within', have never in reality held out much hope of doing so; rather, perhaps, has it been their true intent to use the institutions of the EEC to shape the policy of Europe in their own image.

There has never been a single definitive statement of what are British objectives for policy in the EEC; nor is it wholly reasonable to expect one. It is, however, possible to discern certain fairly clearly defined and consistent strands in British thinking and aspirations about the direction in which policy should go. First and foremost has been the belief that the European Economic Community should primarily concern itself with economic matters. In British eyes the EEC exists essentially to pursue economic objectives.

It is a part of Britain's case that when she joined the Community, economic objectives were the only ones on offer. As I have already suggested, this interpretation of what Britain signed up to is highly debatable. There was a tendency from the beginning for British negotiators in particular to ignore the 'Preambles' to the Treaties they agreed to sign. The 'blurb' before the main articles has consistently been thought by the British to be too 'general' and without sufficient specific meaning to merit much attention. This has not been the view taken by the Roman lawyers in other European countries. The British have overlooked such generalisations in the Treaty of Rome as, 'Determined to lay the foundation of an ever closer union among the peoples of Europe'. They have focused instead on what they have seen to be the 'real' text to which they were committing themselves. This, in their view, has been clear enough: Article 1 of the Rome Treaty states, 'By this Treaty the high contracting parties establish among themselves a EUROPEAN ECONOMIC COMMUNITY'. Article 2 goes on to say,

> The Community shall have as its task, by establishing a common market and progressively approximating the economic policies of Member States, to promote throughout the Community a harmonious development of economic activities, a continuous and balanced expansion, an increase in stability, an accelerated raising of the standard of living and closer relations between the States belonging to it.

Supported almost unanimously by her business and financial community, Britain, in her own eyes, was creating for herself no more and no less than an enormous home market comparable to that of the United States and larger than that of the new trading giant, Japan. This was for her pretty well the end of the matter.

The British view that membership of the EEC was in essence about trade persisted through the signing in 1986 of the Single European Act, though in this case even the main text that was agreed ranged rather wider than the limits that the British had set themselves. Article 1 of the Single European Act reads: 'The European Communities and European Political Cooperation shall have as their objective to contribute together to making concrete progress towards European unity.' The Preamble, needless to say, is even more wide-ranging. Here there is talk of cooperation on foreign policy and of furthering 'the European idea'; there is also seen to be the need to 'protect' Europe's 'common interests' and to invest 'this union with the necessary means of action'. Nevertheless, the British were able to persuade themselves that the Single European Act was essentially about setting a timetable (1 January 1993) and establishing the detailed provisions for a 'single' trading market; as such the 'European idea' remained acceptably circumscribed.

When they came to the Maastricht Treaty on European Union, British negotiators, at least, convinced themselves that they were operating in reasonably acceptable territory. Leaving aside the commitment to the 'duties' of the new 'Union Citizens' (which the genuinely non-Federalists in the British party presumably dismissed as 'meaningless generality'), the main text, according to the British view, was concerned with economic matters. The British party indeed congratulated itself on having fought to keep such matters as foreign and social policy out of that part of the text which in its view constituted the 'genuine' amendments to the Treaty of Rome.

In reality, neither Maastricht nor the Treaties before it were restricted in their impact to economic matters. Enough has been said to indicate how the institutions and the legal system to which Britain acceded have been able, on the back of the Treaty of Rome and its amendments, to stretch their influence far beyond the economic boundaries hoped for and assumed by the British.

The question remains as to whether British policy-makers can fairly argue that by fighting 'from within', although they may not have entirely succeeded in limiting the battleground to issues of trade and markets, they have nevertheless ensured that the economic policy itself has pointed in the right direction.

That there has been a consistent theme to British economic policy over many years is clear; how successfully it has been implemented within the EEC is more obscure.

Representing as they have done the interests of a high-seas trading nation (Britain still exports more per head of population than does Japan), British post-war leaders of all political persuasions, from Nye Bevan to Margaret Thatcher, have largely based their economic policies on the need to expand trade. Furthermore, trade policy has been largely defined by successive governments of both parties in terms of the need to remove barriers to its free development. British economic policy within the EEC has attempted to pursue this theme. The success of Britain's efforts within Europe can therefore largely be judged in terms of the rate at which trade has expanded between Member States, the extent to which this has been based on free and fair competition, and on whether there has been a significant increase in trade between countries of the EEC and the world outside.

Figure 1 makes its own point. EEC trade, as measured at least by exports, has, since British accession, been at a rate of growth of about that of the OECD as a whole – well below that of the newly industrialised countries of Asia and exactly equal to that of the Efta countries. The latter are especially interesting since they constitute the outer ring of the EEC and also because they have considerably higher standards of living than do the EEC Member States.

One of the reasons why there has been nothing outstanding about the rate of growth of trade within the EEC and between the EEC and third countries may have been

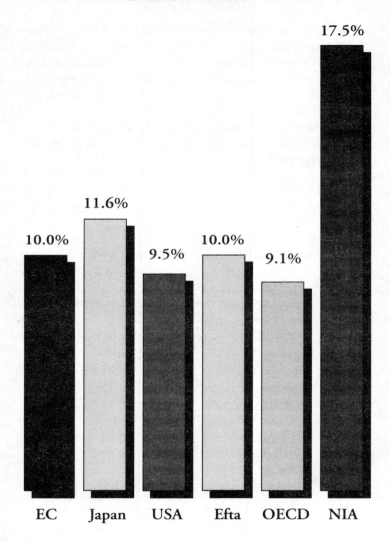

Figure 1 Annual average growth (percentage) in exports by major economic group, 1975–89 (NIA=newly industrialised Asian countries) (source: *IMF*, International Financial Statistics Yearbook, 1991)

because its members have not been as assiduous as might have been expected (by the British at least) in removing barriers to trade between themselves and with the rest of the world. It is true that formal tariffs have in most sectors and between most member countries now been removed. But trade flows are at least as sensitive to the level of non-tariff barriers as they are to tariffs themselves.

Despite the fact that the Common Market has now been in existence for thirty-five years, despite also the fact that its main original *raison d'être* was to abolish obstacles to trade between Member States, a feature of the whole process has been the skill with which countries have managed to keep up their non-tariff trade barriers. The story, in particular of the last ten years or so, could indeed be written entirely in terms of moves towards political union being used as a distraction to divert attention away from the continuing abuse of the commitment to free trade.

The way that the Single European Act of 1986 has been applied is a good example. The British intent when signing this was that it would finally deliver the free-trading and outward-looking 'home' market. The crucial Article 8A inserted into the Treaty of Rome by the Single European Act does indeed state:

> The Community shall adopt measures with the aim of progressively establishing the internal market over a period expiring on 31 December 1992 . . . The internal market shall comprise an area without internal frontiers in which the free movement of goods, persons, services and capital is ensured in accordance with the provisions of the Treaty.

Despite a deadline of 31 December 1992, many of the obstacles to trade – especially in the areas in which Britain excels (banking and investment services, insurance, air travel, shipping and energy production) – remain. This is partly explained by the fact that the countries and institutions that collectively wield the greatest power in the EEC have focused their attention on matters arising out of the Single European Act which have little to do with trade.

Contrary to assessments made by the British at the time of signing, there are many examples of these. Take, for instance, the phrase in Article 8A 'without internal frontiers'. This has been pounced on by Germany, France and by the Commission – not, as the British would wish, further to liberalise trade within the Community, but, for instance, to try to abolish controls on the movement of immigrants. Both Germany and France now have very serious and open-ended immigration obligations (Germany because of very free asylum obligations written into her basic law and France because of citizenship rights bestowed on her former colonies). Germany has in the past year alone accepted some quarter of a million refugees from the former Yugoslavia. The German and French objective, therefore, is to have a common European perimeter border against further immigration and to share the burden arising out of their open-ended commitments by allowing the immigrants they attract to move freely within the EEC.

When Germany, France and the Commission combine, it is virtually impossible to stand in their way. In an attempt to do so, Britain pointed to a General Declaration attached to the Single European Act, which says, 'Nothing in these provisions shall affect the right of Member States to take such measures as they consider necessary for the purpose of controlling immigration . . .' In the event, a compromise was struck. Britain was allowed, in effect, to retain her border controls, subject to certain conditions, while the principle of EEC jurisdiction was conceded. The status of the Declaration remains to be tested in the European Court.

The row about border controls has already served to deflect everybody's mind from the main body and thrust of

Article 8A, which was meant finally to establish the Common Market by the end of 1992. The question, from the point of view of assessing the effectiveness of Britain's involvement at the centre of Europe, is: Has the Single European Act achieved its objectives within the time-scale it set itself?

If one looks at the matter in terms of the number of Directives related to trade and competition issued by the Commission, then undoubtedly there is seen to have been progress. Several hundred Directives associated with competition have now been brought into effect. It is true also that with respect to free trade in some of the more intractable areas (which happen also in many cases to be of greatest interest to Britain) some progress has been made. For instance, there now exists the 'Third Directive for Non-Life and Life Insurance', which will, when it is implemented, ostensibly allow for free trade in insurance. It will not, however, come into effect until 1 July 1994, eighteen months after the deadline laid down by the Single European Act. According to the Council Regulations agreed by transport ministers on 22 June 1992, total free trade in air services between and within countries must wait until 1997; only then will it be possible for airlines to operate freely within particular countries, the so-called 'cabotage' rights.

As for banking services, at the time of writing there is no agreement on the draft Investment Services Directive which deals with trade in services in the securities field. Inevitably in this case there has been agreement on matters to do with regulation and standardisation (the Capital Adequacy Directive), which though no doubt treated as a 'competition directive' is arguably restrictive of it. Indeed, the remaining debate between the British and other Member States on this matter now centres on the question of how much regulation (or restriction on the freedom to trade) there should be for banking services.

In the case of shipping services, at the meeting of

transport ministers in Luxembourg on 22 June 1992, Britain, Denmark and the Netherlands were simply outvoted on the issue of a free market. As a result, there will be restrictions for cruise services until 1995, the transport of strategic goods (oil and water) until 1997, services in ships below 650 gross tonnes until 1998 and regular passenger and ferry services until 1999. Certain services in Greek waters will be protected until the year 2004. Restrictive practices concerned with crewing nationality are to continue for the most part until the end of the century.

British attempts to create a free market in energy, especially in the generation and sale of electricity and in the distribution of gas, have not met with much more success. Proposed Directives were produced on these issues by the Commission before the Council of Ministers on 21 February 1992. The tone of these is not untypical of Commission Directives concerned with the internal market. This is not defined, as the British would wish, in terms of the free flow of competitive trade, but as follows:

> Whereas it is therefore necessary to establish common rules for the licensing by Member States of the construction and operation of the generating installations and transmission and distribution lines and to take such other steps as are required in order to ensure the effective functioning of the internal market.
> Whereas the need to ensure a real opening up of the market and a fair balance in the application of these measures requires the introduction of harmonised criteria and procedures for the construction and operation of generating installations.
> Whereas the establishing of the internal market for energy, more particularly the electricity sector, will take into account the objective of economic and social cohesion.

Everything, in other words, is taken into account except competition between producers and distributors. Towards the end of the Directive this is granted to 'large industrial companies and with regard to the distribution companies under certain conditions'.

The limited nature of the proposed level of competition is itself accepted in the Electricity Directive:

> Whereas these measures constitute a second phase of liberalisation . . . it will be necessary to provide for further market liberalisation including the reduction of barriers to the supply of electricity by producers to customers; whereas the precise details of this third phase, which should complete the internal electricity market, can only be defined in the light of experience . . .

In other words, 'We'll see how we get along before we have any real competition between the sort of independent power producers whom the British are nurturing under their free-market arrangements.'

In any case, for the moment all this is of merely academic interest. Even the very limited amount of competition and market liberalisation proposed in the Electricity and Gas Directives has been too much for the German (highly inefficient) coal-mining interests to swallow. The French would be content so long as the arrangement was for them to *sell* abroad; there can, however, be no question of France permitting her massive investment in nuclear power to be undermined by making it possible for French consumers to buy in from abroad. At the time of writing, therefore, the Electricity and Gas Directives with their very limited objectives (as seen at least through British eyes) are blocked by a majority led by the French and the Germans. The day when Britain's independent power producers will be able to sell competitively and freely into a European grid as a matter of right would seem to be a long way off, despite the fact that this was all supposed to have been in place by the end of 1992.

At the root of the problem is a fundamental difference of approach between Britain and most of her EEC partners. Britain defines it in terms of competition and free trading; most of the other countries conceive of it in terms of minimum operating standards. These, as we now know, involve everything from environmental considerations to limits on the working hours of employees.

I am reminded of the period in the 1980s when I was directly involved in the negotiations on these matters. Whether as Minister for Aviation or as Minister for Coal and Electricity, I had the same experience whenever I arrived at a meeting of the Council of Ministers. The first item on the agenda invariably was a British proposition to remove some barrier to free trade: for instance to remove the pooling arrangements between airlines and to make air fares more freely competitive, or to make electricity grids around Europe more accessible to competing power companies. These proposals were invariably rejected on the grounds of being impractical (in reality because France or Germany wished to protect a state-owned operation: German coal-mines, Air France or Lufthansa). The second item on the agenda, which was quickly approved, was a proposal that the Commission should issue Directives aimed at, for instance, creating minimum pollution or air-safety standards. Item 3 was the press release saying, in effect, how unhelpful the British had been. Item 4 was the agreement to give subsidies to the Irish, the Portuguese and the Greeks.

This, it may be argued, is something of a caricature. And, as we have seen, on the face of it things have moved on a little in the direction that the British would wish. Or have they? Does the agreement by EEC states, albeit belated and as yet incomplete, to a series of apparently liberal Directives on competition and trade add up to a victory for the British view of what the Single Market should be about?

In order to answer this, it is first necessary to consider the structure of the industrial and services sectors in the countries of the EEC. Particularly interesting are the organisations providing utility services: gas, electricity, water and transportation. These are for the most part state-owned or Government-controlled in all EEC countries other than the United Kingdom. The same is true of much of banking and, indeed, of manufacturing industry.

The fact that the state is the guarantor of these undertakings puts them in a totally different trading position from that of their genuinely independent British counterparts. This difference is not a new phenomenon. It has been true for years of much of manufacturing (completely differentiating the position of, for instance, Peugeot–Renault in France from British Leyland, or Bull from ICL).

The privatisation during the 1980s of all the major British utilities has brought out into the open the whole question of the preferential treatment given by EEC institutions to publicly owned as against private organisations. The power enjoyed in every sense by, for instance, the state-owned Électricité de France puts it into a completely different position from that of the British National Power or of Powergen. It is highly relevant to an assessment of the likelihood of creating a free market for electricity in Europe (whatever the ambitions of the appropriate Directive) that the French state-owned monopolist generating company also controls the electricity grid. This in itself makes it improbable that independent producers of energy will have free access to the French grid. The position in the United Kingdom is very different. Even were it so minded, the privately owned National Grid Company would be prohibited from arbitrarily preventing access to its system, by both the terms of the Electricity Act of 1989 (which I had the honour to pilot through Parliament) and by the electricity

67

regulatory body, OFFER (Office of Electricity Regulation).

Nor is it simply a question of the structural differences between British industry and much of its Continental counterpart. There is no doubt that officialdom in Brussels turns a blind eye to anti-competitive behaviour by state-owned industries in a way that it is not prepared to do for private companies. It is certainly one of the ironies for Britain that the more thorough her privatisation programme in the 1980s (including gas, electricity, air transport and telecommunications), the more disadvantaged she became in the argument for pan-European liberalisation of trade.

Part of the reason for this is that the forces which dominate proceedings in Brussels place greater emphasis on common standards (which they often confuse with higher standards), in preference to the provision of a framework which is genuinely competitive. Whether this flows from a suspicion of private undertakings which lurks in every large bureaucracy, or whether it is out of a deeper political distaste for what Britain has done, or from a misguided belief that state-owned organisations are cleaner and safer than private ones, is unclear.

What is certain is that in the EEC there is literally one law for the private company and another for the state-owned one. Nowhere does this manifest itself more blatantly than in the way that the state, in most EEC countries, is allowed by EEC institutions to use the enterprises it owns or controls to act as vehicles for receiving and in some cases dispensing subsidies. These are handed out by EEC governments, other than the British, on a massive scale to their industry. They make a mockery of the notion that there exists within the Community a free market or even that there is one in the offing. The most notable example in 1992 was the 6.6 billion francs received by Groupe Bull from the French taxpayer.

The story of what is going on in the airline industry will perhaps provide as good an example as any of the gap which is growing between what is proposed in the 'competition Directives' and how matters are likely to work out in practice as a result of the distortions caused by subsidy.

The Air Services regulation agreed and signed by the Council of Transport Ministers in Luxembourg on 22 June 1992 was certainly clear in its intent: 'Whereas air fares should normally be determined freely by market forces . . .' it begins; with respect to the question of access of competing airlines to particular routes, it continues, 'Whereas it is necessary to abolish restrictions concerning multiple designation . . .'

In other words, airlines are to be able to compete freely, charging fares they judge to be appropriate, so long as these are not predatory and the result of cross-subsidisation. I would have given my right arm to have achieved such an agreement when I was Minister for Aviation between 1984 and 1987. It was not, I may say, for want of trying, but in my day it eluded me. If all went well with the Air Services package agreed in June 1992, EEC airlines would be able to fly between whatever airports in different countries within the Community they chose (subject only to complying with safety and noise standards and assuming the availability of ground and air space) and charging the economic fares they chose. Air fares, still outrageously high in Europe compared, for instance, to those across the Atlantic, would fall and the market for air travel would expand. After 1997, subject to certain registration restrictions, all this would apply to flights within, as well as to those between, countries.

Almost on the same day that the third package Air Services Regulation was signed by the governments of the EEC, the state-owned Banque de Paris injected £128 million of cash into Air France in what it said was a 'normal' financial transaction. Normality in this context is open to several different interpretations. It may be standard practice in France for one state enterprise to give to another large sums of money when one of them is in financial trouble; but it is doubtful whether private undertakings would have considered this particular transaction as 'normal'.

It took place immediately after Air France had turned in a loss of 685 million francs. From the airline's point of view, the gift (disguised as an 8.8 per cent investment stake by BNP) could therefore not have been more conveniently timed. Not only did it meet the airline's losses without the latter suffering any real penalty, but it enabled it to pursue its plans to take a 6 billion franc (37.5 per cent) shareholding in the Belgian state-owned carrier Sabena, which was in an equally parlous financial state.

The fact that the Commission sat on its hands and did nothing during these events must be taken as some indication of the prevailing mood in Brussels. It certainly explains why Lufthansa, Alitalia and Iberia, each of whose accounts is largely hidden from public scrutiny, will continue to cross-subsidise their operations, and when necessary receive financial support from their sponsoring governments. Despite the best intent of the Air Services Regulations, each airline will therefore be extremely well placed to 'fight off' any intrusive and unwelcome competition.

The financial guarantees and direct support provided by most Member States to their nationalised companies are likely to affect the impact of many of the 'competition Directives', however well-meaning these may be. The effect of, for instance, the Banking and Energy Directives will undoubtedly be diluted in this way.

In the case of the Electricity and Gas Directives (assuming they eventually come into force) there is the added factor that the nationalised monopolist is likely to be closely involved in determining the crucial safety and security issues. Where, for instance, an independent power generator will be permitted by Directive to plug into the grid of any Member State (something, as we have seen, not actually proposed by the Commission at present), it will be able to do so only with a safety clearance from the appropriate 'home' authority. In the French case, for example, the regulatory body is likely to be none other than Électricité de France or one which relies for 'technical' advice almost exclusively on the state-owned monopoly. It does not take much imagination to conjure up the kinds of arguments that EDF will introduce should it wish to inhibit serious competition to itself. I had them all myself from the former British monopoly, the Central Electricity Generating Board, when I was the minister responsible for the day-to-day operations involved in privatising the British electricity industry: 'the integrity of the system', the need to ensure the adequacy of contra power or 'vars', safety considerations, the impossibility of storing electricity – all excellent points in themselves, but each fully capable of being accommodated in a competitive system such as has been invented, at least in embryo, in Britain. Here there exists a political will pressing for the development of competitive markets; this would seem not to be present to the same extent among the other Member States of the EEC.

I have focused on services and utilities because these tend to have been the most recent to be covered by 'liberalising' Directives and agreements. The argument applies just as forcibly to many manufacturing industries, such as those of automobiles, electronic components, computers and aircraft. Each of these industries on the continent of Europe is to a greater or lesser extent owned or controlled by the state, and when it suits the authorities to do so, is heavily subsidised. Often it is another state-owned body which is used to provide the mechanism for making the payment; this, as we have seen, provides a way of dressing up the deal as being commercially 'normal'. An example was the operation in 1992 by the Commission d'Énergie Atomique to feed cash into the ailing electronics giant Thomson CSF.

71

The idea that there is free trade in the EEC is in many key sectors of economic activity as misplaced as would be the suggestion that there is a free market in European agricultural products, another sector which it has been British policy to attempt to liberalise.

For these reasons, an analysis of the so-called 'uneven playing-field' in Europe does not need to dwell for too long on the fact that there remains in many countries a low level of compliance with the rules. It is true that rule-breaking is a national pastime in a country like Italy; but that is a problem which is no doubt capable of being resolved by a European government with sufficient teeth. Under Maastricht (Article 104C), it is, for instance, proposed that the authorities in Brussels should be able to impose fines on countries which do not obey the edicts of EEC institutions.

The problem of the uneven playing-field goes much deeper than those arising from non-compliance. At its root it is explained by a divergence of certain fundamental objectives between different Member States. This poses a particular problem for Britain with her emphasis on the free-trading potential of the EEC, an objective which is not given similar prominence by her fellow Members. It is certainly not reflected within the institutions of the EEC. There the emphasis on standards is more in the German tradition. It reflects, for instance, the attitudes fostered by the German standards office through the DIN (the Deutsche Industrie-Norm, or Industrial Standard). This organisation happily ploughs a furrow totally at odds with the notion of free trade, by making it as difficult as possible for non-German companies to sell their wares in Germany without DIN approval – even where EEC law says that the only approval necessary is from the country of origin.

The problem, in other words, for the British in arguing their case for free trade is that they are up against a deep cultural divide which separates them from most of the other Member States. It is a difference which explains why

Britain alone has privatised most of her industry, whereas her neighbours have not; and why she spends 1.1 per cent of her gross national product on industrial subsidies while her partners spend 3 to 4 per cent of theirs.

Britain is quite simply outnumbered in her view that the EEC is essentially a trading venture. For most of the others, the association is not even primarily economic, but political. Each, it is true, has her own perspective: for France, it is about cocking a snook at the Americans, for Germany about playing the leading role in a superstate, for Italy about compensating for her chronic democratic weaknesses; for others it is to be able to benefit from German largesse. Only for the British, the Danes and, to a lesser extent, the Dutch, is it about commerce.

Not only does this constrain Britain's ability to win the internal-trade argument, it makes her position less than dominant on the question of Europe's attitude to the development of trade with third countries. The performance of the EEC during the Uruguay round of GATT discussions was instructive and probably a foretaste of what is to come. Whereas Britain took it as axiomatic that the objective of these negotiations was to reduce the general level of tariff barriers as a matter of good economic principle, her partners in Europe have viewed the matter from the other end of the telescope. They have believed that the whole purpose of the EEC is to build protective barriers which should only be reduced in return for a high price to be paid by 'the other side'. This attitude has certainly prevailed in negotiations with the Americans over the question of agricultural protection. (I am not arguing that the Americans do not themselves engage in all manner of protectionist devices, but merely note that they do at least have an intrinsic belief in the benefits of Adam Smith's hidden hand, a view which is not wholly shared on the Continent of Europe.) The protectionist attitude of the majority of EEC members has also prevailed, sadly, with respect to trade with the former eastern-bloc countries of Europe.

One is led to conclude from all this that despite some tactical 'victories' here and there, the British point of view with respect to policy in the EEC has not on the whole prevailed, any more than has its influence over the development of the institutional framework of the Community.

It is quite possible, however, even if her influence within the EEC has been weak, that Britain has nevertheless gained great benefits from her membership. It may be that Britain has overemphasised the potential benefits of free trade; that she has actually benefited from the protectionist philosophy which permeates the EEC; that being a member of a cohesive new power bloc is what has counted; that the 'fight' with the Americans over agricultural matters is a case in point; that had she been on her own, Britain would have been trampled over by her cousins on the other side of the Atlantic.

The statement that 'Britain cannot afford to go it alone' is usually presented as a matter of fact, as a point so strong as to be undebatable. Perhaps the time has come to test it. To what extent is it founded on hard evidence? What, indeed, have been the measurable (especially economic) benefits of Britain's membership of the EEC?

Chapter 5

The Economic Impact on Britain of EEC Membership

1. CASH COSTS

FOR BRITAIN the argument for membership of the EEC has pivoted from the start around its perceived economic benefits to her. British industry, the City of London, most of what used to be called Fleet Street, and the economic spokesmen for all the political parties have for many years spoken with one voice on this matter: what Britain required, they all said, was a large, secure home market in which it was possible to benefit from economies of scale comparable to those enjoyed by the Japanese and the Americans. To this view in recent years has been added the opinion that great benefits would be attached to stabilising Britain's currency by linking it to the Deutschmark.

The judgement as to the potential trading benefits to Britain has been vindicated in at least one sense. By the end of the 1980s the countries of the EEC collectively became the recipients of over half Britain's exports. By 1988 Britain was for the first time selling more to the EEC than to the rest of the world (£47 billion out of £93.5 billion at 1991 prices). It is true that Europe was taking the bulk of British exports in part because of the fall-off in sales to the United States, which was entering a period of recession, but the importance of her sales within Europe was self-evident.

There has, however, been a very high price to pay for the opportunity offered by this large 'home market'.

For a start, Britain has to an extent been forced by the rules and practices of the EEC artificially to divert her exporting efforts to Europe and away from where they may have been more beneficially employed for her in the rest of the world.

This has been brought about in two ways, first, by specific EEC Directives which insist, for instance, that Britain gives preference to EEC countries with respect to her sales of North Sea oil. Second, British exporters are the victims of a generally restrictive and protectionist EEC posture with respect to world trade. This has come to a head with EEC obstructionist moves at the Uruguay round of GATT negotiations which were meant to reach a conclusion by 1990 but which would now appear to have collapsed.

An indication of what would be Britain's natural pattern of trade were she not in part restricted by her membership of the EEC is given by the fact that less than 20 per cent of her foreign investment currently goes to the countries of the EEC. Figure 1 (see page 60) certainly makes it very clear that the EEC is by no means the best market in terms of growth for Britain to be selling into.

Even (some might say especially) in purely trading terms, Britain has been paying a very high price for her membership of the EEC. This is readily apparent when one considers not export patterns alone, though they themselves have been distortive to an extent, but Britain's balance of trade with the EEC countries.

Since she joined the Common Market in 1972, Britain has suffered a sharp deterioration in her balance of trade in manufactures with the other Member States. From a surplus of £385 million in 1970, Britain had reached an annual deficit of £3,410 million by 1979, as seen in Chapter 2.

Between 1981 and 1991 the United Kingdom ran an overall deficit of some £80,000 million with the EEC. Over the same period Britain was in surplus with the rest of the world to the tune of £78,000 million. In 1990 alone the deficit with the EEC was £13,000 million (some £30 million per day); with the rest of the world Britain's surplus in 1990 was £2,000 million. These deficit figures do not include levies paid on non-EEC imports, net capital outflow, or the loss of Commonwealth and Efta market preferences.

To the cost to Britain of membership of the EEC on her trade account must be added what she pays for the Common Agricultural Policy (CAP).

Provision for the establishment of a common agricultural policy was made in Articles 39 and 40 of the Treaty of Rome. It was a *sine qua non* of French participation in the EEC, and thus of the very formation of an EEC.

Negotiations on the precise shape and form of the CAP took four years and it was – unsurprisingly – the protectionist view of France and her allies which emerged triumphant in January 1962. The principles agreed at its inception continue to govern the CAP today: farm product prices are determined annually and maintained by intervention and export subsidies; protection from external produce is operated by variable import levies; and financial responsibility is implemented through the European Agricultural Guidance and Guarantee Fund. Despite frequent calls for the profligate spending on agriculture to be reined in, the CAP continues to absorb around two-thirds of the EEC budget.

The burden which the CAP places upon taxpayers and consumers is enormous. Taxpayers pay the equivalent of over £60 for each person in the EEC to the CAP budget each year (*Consumers and the Common Agricultural Policy*, National

Consumer Council, 1988). As consumers, every citizen in the EEC pays £122 per year in artificially high food prices (*National Policies and Agricultural Trade: Study on the EEC*, OECD, 1987). A typical European family of four is thus being forced to pay almost £1,000 per year, or above £18 per week. This burden falls most heavily upon the poorest people, whose expenditure on food represents a larger proportion of their income, and is mainly directed at those foods which the CAP taxes most.

With most forms of taxation, there is the consolidation of contributing towards a social purpose. In the case of the CAP, the taxpayer is supporting a system which is unmatched in its waste, its inefficiency and its harmful social, economic and environmental effects. There is no intrinsic benefit gained from paying farmers not to produce food, or from paying for food to be stored and destroyed rather than sold at a fair market price. Even as a mechanism for transferring wealth to farmers, the CAP is inefficient. For every £100 contributed by taxpayers and consumers, European farmers receive some £62 (*Consumers and the Common Agricultural Policy*, NCC, 1988). In Britain, which suffers most from the CAP, the cost of support is around double the gain to British farmers (Richard Howarth, *The Common Agricultural Policy*). Moreover, blanket support by volume of output ensures that most of the support goes to the wealthiest 25 per cent of landowners, who produce 75 per cent of output.

The indirect effects of the CAP are no less damaging.

First, by denying fair trade to developing countries whose economies rely upon agriculture, the CAP is directly responsible for much of the poverty in the Third World (A. Moyes, *How Farming in Europe Affects the Third World*, Oxfam, 1986). The same is true of the tough stance taken by the EEC against agricultural imports from Eastern Europe's emerging democracies.

Second, the EEC's retention of its subsidy policy in agriculture is the chief obstacle to agreement at the GATT talks and thus to freeing the world trading system, including providing new markets for British farmers.

Third, the CAP absorbs resources wastefully, thus creating a 'massive misallocation of resources in the EEC economy' (*Consumers and the Common Agricultural Policy*, NCC, 1988). Countries like Britain, which might benefit from different allocations of the budget to which they contribute so disproportionately, are thus penalised both positively and negatively.

Fourth, enforced high food prices have increased inflation, worsened the competitive position of the whole economy and contributed to rising unemployment, without benefiting agriculture commensurately.

And fifth, the types of subsidy encourage a further depletion of environmental resources: hedgerows are destroyed, woods felled and chemical fertilisers employed in pursuit of output-based hand-outs from the CAP budget.

The CAP is significant in what it represents as much as in its own failings. It demonstrates the principle that the EEC's worst-managed and least successful policies are those in which it has unrestrained jurisdiction. The track record of the CAP raises serious questions over the ability of the organs of the EEC to wield the powers which they have gained.

The third form of cash costs to Britain of her membership of the EEC is the direct payments she makes into the central budget.

The EEC has evolved a mechanism for raising revenue known as 'own resources'. This derives from the proceeds of the Common External Tariff and agricultural import levies, a VAT component and a resource based upon the gross national products of the Member States. It is this last which, at the time of writing, is proving to be a major issue of contention in Council meetings, as the Commission and its allies demand a considerable increase in order to fund a further transfer of wealth to the EEC's poorer nations as part of the 'Cohesion Fund'.

Growth in the size of the EEC budget has accelerated in a steady curve over the last three decades. At the time of Britain's accession in 1973, the budget stood at £2,000 million per annum; in 1991 it had risen to over £43,000 million.

As Figure 2 shows, the United Kingdom has been a large net contributor to the EEC budget. Britain's fight for better budgeting terms dominated much of the debate within the EEC for the first ten years of British membership, masking the more important questions of sovereignty and Federalism. Margaret Thatcher managed to negotiate a system of rebates at the Fontainebleau Summit in 1984, but the British contribution remains wholly out of proportion to the size of her economy. Her net contribution to the EEC budget now stands at well over £2 billion every year – a cost equivalent to that of building over a hundred National Health Service hospitals. Not only is this figure certain to rise as spending on 'Cohesion' increases, but there are even calls, led by Germany, for the proportion paid by the United Kingdom to be increased further.

Augmenting Britain's direct contributions to the EEC are numerous ways in which specific British resources are made available for common EEC exploitation. One of the most notorious examples of this is the Common Fisheries Policy introduced – significantly – in 1971. Under the terms of this policy, Britain, which possessed 60 per cent of EEC fish stocks, was allocated a quota which reduced its share to 30 per cent. Since then the quota has been further reduced to the extent where the British fishing industry is very seriously threatened. The European Court has recently ruled that the reduced share which Britain has been allowed to retain may now be fished by boats from other EEC countries which take the trouble to register as British companies.

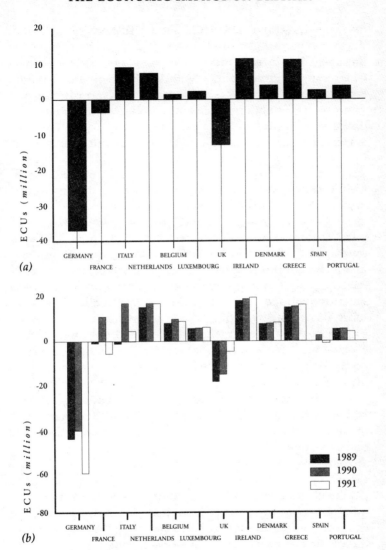

Figure 2 *Average net position of EC Members in Community Budget, (a) 1980–91 and (b) 1989–91* (source: *Mark Bainbridge and Brian Burkitt, Department of Social and Economic Studies, University of Bradford)*

81

2. TOWARDS A SINGLE CURRENCY?

Sufficient has already been said to suggest that Britain's economic and financial ties with the EEC are much more complex than those of a simple trading relationship, even one which for a variety of reasons involves considerable net outflows of cash.

Increasingly, membership of the EEC requires of Britain that she accept the imposition of economic regulation. Specifically, during the 1980s this has meant progressively losing control over economic policy in return for merging her currency with those of her EEC partners.

With the collapse of Britain's membership of the European Exchange Rate Mechanism on Wednesday, 16 September 1992, the trend towards monetary integration was in theory temporarily halted. However, the Government made it plain that they intended to go back into the ERM when they judged the moment to be right. Indeed, by the terms of Article 109J(i) of the Treaty of Maastricht (to which Britain's opt-out does not apply) they were bound to do so. It remains highly appropriate therefore to assess the impact on the British economy of fixing its currency to those of the other countries of the EEC.

How is one to measure the net economic impact on Britain of her recent membership of the ERM? Ultimately it must come down to taking a view of what effect it has had on the standard of living of her people.

There are many 'indicators' for assessing how well off the people of a nation are becoming: growth in output, output per head, inflation and productivity are four of them. A quick glance at Table 1 will show that by these measures the three major countries of the EEC, including Britain, have on the whole fared progressively worse through the period of their membership of the EEC. All three did badly compared to Japan and performed roughly on a level with the United States. Britain performed particularly badly in the 1970s

Table 1 Rates of change in economic indicators in selected countries, historical data (percentage per annum)

Period	United Kingdom	France	West Germany[1]	United States	Japan[2]
(A) GDP at constant prices					
1950–60	2.8	4.6	8.0	3.2	8.0
1960–70	2.9	5.6	4.5	3.8	10.5
1970–80	1.9	3.2	2.7	2.7	4.9
1980–90	2.6	2.2	2.1	2.9	4.2
(B) GDP per head at constant prices					
1950–60	2.4	3.6	6.9	1.5	6.9
1960–70	2.2	4.5	3.6	2.5	9.3
1970–80	1.8	2.6	2.5	1.7	3.6
1980–90	2.4	1.7	1.8	1.9	3.6
(C) GDP deflator					
1950–60	4.2	6.7	3.0	2.5	3.8
1960–70	4.2	4.4	3.7	3.0	5.4
1970–80	14.0	9.9	5.3	7.4	7.4
1980–90	6.3	6.4	2.9	4.2	1.7
(D) Manufacturing output per hour					
1950–60	n.a.	n.a.	n.a.	n.a.	n.a.
1960–70	3.7	6.7	5.7	2.8	10.8
1970–80	2.4	4.5	3.9	2.3	5.9
1980–90	4.9	3.5	2.4	2.5	4.1

Notes: 1. Data for 1950–60 exclude the Saar and West Berlin.

2. Data for Japan in the 1950s are for 1952–60 only.

Sources: OECD: (1) *National Accounts 1960 to 1990*, Vol. 1. (2) *National Accounts 1950 to 1978*, Vol. 1. (3) *Main Economic Indicators*, July 1992. CSO, *Economic Trends Annual Supplement*, 1991. IMF, *International Financial Statistics*, 1989 Yearbook. *One Hundred Years of Economic Statistics*, The Economist Publications. US Department of Labor, *Monthly Labor Review*, December 1991.

immediately after she joined the Common Market, especially in terms of growth in output and of her annual
average rate of inflation. She put up a better show in the
1980s. However, when one turns to the year-by-year figures
in Table 2, the picture, even for that period, becomes more
variable. After a shaky start at the beginning of the decade,
the British economy began to grow fast in the middle years
of the period. The rates of increase in productivity were
particularly impressive at that time. Growth began to slow
down sharply in 1989 and, coincidentally, inflation started
to rise.

The disastrous years for the British economy, measured
in terms of change in real wealth, were 1990, 1991 and 1992
('growth' for 1992 is now estimated at around minus 2.0 per
cent as opposed to the Treasury's original forecast of plus
1 per cent). These years coincided precisely with Britain's membership of the European Exchange Rate Mechanism (ERM). During these three years there was also a
sharp deterioration in Britain's balance of trade, not
assisted by her annual average deficit on her trade account
with the EEC of some £10 billion. One unfortunate side-
effect of the decline in both her 'visible' and 'invisible'
balance was that a dramatic change occurred in Britain's net
overseas assets. In 1986 these had stood at £99.4 billion; by
the beginning of 1992 they had fallen to £16 billion.

It is sometimes said that this appalling performance by
the British economy in the early 1990s has been 'imported'
from a world recession. The facts do not bear out this
theory. British exports as a whole have, in fact, continued to
rise throughout the period, both in value and volume
terms. The problem of the trade balance is caused by the
fact that imports have risen at an even faster rate, a most
unusual phenomenon during such a severe recession.

Unusual, perhaps, but not inexplicable. Britain's recent
balance-of-payments problems have to date had very little
to do with the general level of world demand and almost

everything to do with the ability of foreign companies to introduce their products into the country at competitive prices. This is in turn largely explained by a sharp deterioration in Britain's unit costs relative to those of her competitors which, until 16 September 1992, was not reflected in a change in the exchange value of the pound. The sterling/Deutschmark rate would seem to have been particularly out of kilter when account is taken of the rise in Britain's unit costs against those of Germany. Britain's exports to the EEC have been expensive and her imports cheap.

The British authorities argued at the time that the way to tackle this problem of falling competitiveness, far from being to allow the pound to devalue, was to maintain a rigid exchange rate for sterling and so through the resulting high interest rates and tight money 'to squeeze inflation out of the system'.

Britain therefore experienced a credit squeeze in the early 1990s during a period of recession in much the same way – and for much the same reasons – that she experienced a credit boom during the period of growth and 'overheating' in the mid-1980s. On each occasion exchange-rate policy took precedence over the introduction of monetary and fiscal policy appropriate to the needs of the economy. On the first occasion, the effect was to build up worrying inflationary pressures; on the second, it was to create more bankruptcies, higher unemployment, lower investment (thus higher unit costs) and, arguably – with a persistent tendency for wage costs to continue to rise – higher, not lower, inflation. This last point is important. As investment has slowed down, so have productivity rates. Distortions and rigidities in the labour market have meant that rising unemployment has not been accompanied by a matching fall in wage rates. This, and faltering output, has meant a rise in unit costs. It is in this sense, and by the high price it attaches to capital, that high interest rates have been inflationary.

Table 2 Rates of change in economic indicators in selcted countries, recent data (percentage per annum)

Period	1980	1981	1982	1983	1984	1985
(A) GDP at constant prices						
United Kingdom	−2.2	−1.3	1.7	3.7	2.2	3.6
France	1.4	1.2	2.3	0.8	1.5	1.8
West Germany	1.1	0.2	−0.9	1.6	2.8	1.9
USA	−0.1	2.3	−2.6	3.9	7.2	3.8
Japan	3.6	3.6	3.2	2.7	4.3	5.0
(B) GDP per head at constant prices						
United Kingdom	−2.3	−1.4	1.8	3.6	2.0	3.3
France	0.9	0.6	1.7	0.3	1.1	1.4
West Germany	0.7	0.0	−0.9	1.9	3.2	2.1
USA	−1.3	1.2	−3.6	2.9	6.2	2.8
Japan	2.8	2.8	2.5	2.0	3.6	4.3
(C) GDP deflator						
United Kingdom	19.5	11.4	7.5	5.4	4.5	5.7
France	11.6	11.3	12.0	9.7	7.3	5.8
West Germany	4.9	4.1	4.4	3.5	2.2	2.1
USA	9.1	9.5	6.4	3.4	3.6	2.7
Japan	4.5	3.8	1.6	1.5	2.3	1.5
(D) Manufacturing output per hour						
United Kingdom	−0.3	5.1	5.8	8.4	5.2	3.3
France	0.8	3.1	7.1	2.5	2.0	4.1
West Germany	−2.0	2.1	−0.5	5.3	3.4	3.7
USA	−0.7	1.3	2.1	5.0	4.8	4.4
Japan	3.7	3.7	4.7	1.9	4.1	5.6

Table 2 contd

Period	1986	1987	1988	1989	1990	1991
(A) GDP at constant prices						
United Kingdom	3.9	4.8	4.2	2.3	0.8	−2.2
France	2.4	2.2	3.8	3.6	2.6	1.3
West Germany	2.2	1.4	3.7	3.3	4.7	3.1
USA	3.2	3.5	4.5	2.8	0.9	−0.7
Japan	2.6	4.1	6.2	4.7	5.2	4.5
(B) GDP per head at constant prices						
United Kingdom	3.7	4.5	4.0	2.0	−0.5	n.a.
France	2.0	1.7	3.4	3.1	2.1	n.a.
West Germany	2.2	1.4	3.0	2.3	2.8	n.a.
USA	2.2	2.5	3.5	1.8	0.1	n.a.
Japan	2.0	3.6	5.8	4.2	5.3	n.a.
(C) GDP deflator						
United Kingdom	3.5	4.9	6.5	7.1	6.4	6.9
France	5.2	2.9	2.9	3.1	3.1	3.0
West Germany	3.3	1.9	1.5	2.6	3.4	4.6
USA	2.7	3.2	3.9	4.4	4.1	3.7
Japan	1.8	0.0	0.4	1.9	2.1	1.9
(D) Manufacturing output per hour						
United Kingdom	4.1	6.1	5.5	4.8	0.8	n.a.
France	1.8	2.0	6.7	4.8	1.0	n.a.
West Germany	0.5	−1.6	3.5	4.3	3.5	n.a.
USA	4.5	5.3	4.5	0.9	2.5	n.a.
Japan	−1.5	8.3	6.0	5.1	3.8	n.a.

Sources: US Department of Labor, *Monthly Labor Review*, December 1991. OECD: (1) *Main Economic Indicators*, July 1992. (2) *National Accounts 1960–1990* (on diskette).

I have to say that all this was relatively easy to predict. I myself did so continuously through 1990. In February 1990, while I was still Minister for Housing, I wrote to the Chancellor of the Exchequer: 'There must be a danger now of a demand squeeze turning into a real threat to supply-side confidence. There seems now to be a lag of about two years between a major change of interest-rate levels and investment rates.'

Seven months later, on 28 September 1990, I wrote to the same Chancellor of the Exchequer:

I have been asking myself again why it is that the UK continues to suffer worse swings of 'stop–go' economic cycles than any of our competitors, with more serious effects in particular on business confidence.

The answer I believe continues to be that our economic and monetary authorities have less of an appreciation than others of the lags in the economy in particular between changes in interest policy and business investment.

They tend, as they have done for the past fifty years, to respond to the events of the day without projecting forward the effects of their policies for the necessary 18–24 months. These policies are therefore alternately more severe and more lax than is required.

Thus, for instance, high interest rates, introduced when the economy was already entering a down swing (and when inflationary forces were mostly caused by a slowdown of productivity increases) will begin seriously to bite as the economy enters a recession next year.

The two arguments against reducing interest rates are now (1) inflation and (2) the pound. Inflation will be brought under control by the emerging recession. A pound related to genuine market conditions is surely what is required for our balance of payments. For this reason I have been convinced for some months that interest rates are too high and that they should start to be reduced at once.

A few days later Britain formalised the relationship between her currency and those of the other members of the EEC, in particular the Deutschmark, by joining the European Exchange Rate Mechanism.

I can only say I took some heart in all of this from the following interchange which had taken place on 1 May between my good friend Sir Patrick McNair-Wilson (Member of Parliament for the New Forest) and the prime minister, Margaret Thatcher. Referring to the meeting which had just taken place in Dublin, Sir Patrick addressed the House of Commons thus:

May I warmly congratulate my right hon. Friend both on her statement this afternoon and on all the ways in which she works for the British interest both in Europe and elsewhere in the world? In her discussion on the exchange rate mechanism, was she aware of the growing unease of many of the member countries about a fixed exchange rate mechanism covering such a broad spectrum when there is so much uncertainty about German monetary union? Is there really a good case for returning to fixed exchange rates after this country's unhappy experience from 1949 to the early 1970s? Therefore, are we not wise in being extremely cautious before we hand over our money supply to a third party?

The prime minister: My hon. Friend has put his finger on an important point. It is one thing to join an exchange rate mechanism with certain quite wide

89

margins within which the currency can fluctuate, as has been necessary. We should consider Spain's experience since joining the exchange rate mechanism because that has not been an easy option for Spain. It would be much more unwise to go to locked exchange rates. Some of us remember the times of fixed exchange rates under the Bretton Woods system when we used to hear in the House details of public expenditure cuts, of how we had to let go a great deal of our reserves, and of high interest rates – all at once. Those problems arose from the fixed Bretton Woods exchange rate system. It was broken, and we should be wary of returning to such a rigid system.

I left the government on 30 November 1990. After that I felt free to express my anxieties more openly. On 6 December, in my first speech for several years from the back benches of the House of Commons, I said: 'Our entry into the ERM was welcomed by both sides of the House and by most of the press, but it is now clear that the bands within which the pound is allowed to float are sustained only by damagingly high rates of interest in Britain.'

This was followed by letters to *The Times* and the *Daily Telegraph* and, a year later, by an anniversary letter to *The Times*.

To the Editor of The Times, *18 December 1990*:

Sir, You said in your leader of 14 December, 'the highly political decision to enter the European exchange rate mechanism last October and at an exchange rate of DM2.95 to the pound looked like a mistake at the time. Today this can no longer be doubted . . .'

I agree and said as much in the House of Commons two weeks ago. The crucial point for this country is the link between the present ERM bands and British interest rates.

Treasury ministers argue that the present levels of interest rates are part of a policy of reducing inflation. This position is now indefensible. Inflation was caused by excess money supply and too low interest rates in 1987–8. Inflation is now crumbling, as it was bound to do because of the recession.

Just as low interest rates some three years ago caused inflationary pressure last year, so continued high interest rates now could turn the recession into a full-blown slump next year or the year after. The true purpose of high interest rates now is not to reduce inflation but to maintain the position negotiated for sterling within the ERM.

The grave prospect is that as German interest rates rise to pay for the reconstruction of the East, so our interest rates will be dragged up further. The government cannot allow this to take place. Sterling must be uncoupled from its present relationship with the D-Mark. We must renegotiate the ERM bands and cut our interest rates at once.

The effect of not doing so is the likelihood that the Conservative Party would lose the next election on the back of a gravely wounded economy.

To the Editor of the Daily Telegraph, *8 January 1991:*

Sir, Your editorial (7 January) argues that a realignment of sterling within the ERM would necessarily be inflationary. Not true.

The question is, if the pound fell in value against the Deutschmark, would we spend more on more expensive foreign goods? The answer depends on the level of our purchasing power and on what economists call elasticities of demand. In the present recession a fall in the value of the pound would not mean a rise in expenditures abroad. It would probably result in a switch to cheaper British goods. It would therefore be anti-inflationary.

Furthermore, if a fall in the pound coincided with a fall in interest rates, leading to a rise in investment and productivity to match current wage demands, this too would be anti-inflationary. Low interest rates are inflationary only when they coincide with an over-heating economy as they did in 1987–8.

The more fundamental point about exchange rates is that they should not be maintained at artificial levels as is certainly the case at present, when sterling has to be supported by 14 per cent interest rates.

Of course you are absolutely right to emphasise the crucial importance of bringing down inflation; the current deep recession will achieve this. With continued high interest and sterling exchange rates we are going for overkill, with grave potential consequences for the economy of this country.

To the Editor of The Times, *27 December 1991*

Sir, A year ago, almost to the day (18 December 1990) you published a letter in which I wrote:

'. . . continued high interest rates now could turn the recession into a full-blown slump . . . The grave prospect is that as German interest rates rise . . . so our interest rates will be dragged up further. The government cannot allow this to take place. Sterling must be uncoupled from its present relationship with the D-Mark. We must renegotiate the ERM bands and cut our interest rates at once . . .'

Since that was written our interest rates have risen *in real terms* to an all-time peak. It would now be an act of political madness further to raise them to support the pound (as indeed it would be to sacrifice more of our reserves to the same purpose).

Last year there was at least the argument that high interest rates were about getting inflation down (a view I disputed at the time). Now a rise in interest rates would be seen in its true colours, as a means for attempting to support the value of sterling at an artificially high level against the D-Mark within the ERM.

Periodic bouts of fixed or artificially determined exchange rates have been the curse of this country for almost a hundred years – by pricing our goods out of world markets and, through high interest rates, by forcing up the cost of capital here.

I pray that my colleagues in government will see the sense of now taking the pressure off British interest rates. At the very least this will mean their preparing for a general realignment of the ERM currencies.

Given the predictable economic consequences of Britain's entry into the ERM, the question is, why was it done? More fundamentally, why as early as 1987 did the then Chancellor of the Exchequer, Nigel Lawson, adopt the policy of 'informally' linking the exchange value of the pound to that of the Deutschmark?

There would seem in retrospect to have been two primary reasons. The first, and perhaps most logical – though one that is vigorously denied by Lord Lawson – is that it was part of a move leading to full monetary union and a Single Currency in Europe. If this was not the primary motivation within the Treasury, then it certainly was amongst those in the Foreign and Commonwealth Office who were keen not to be 'out of step' in Europe. Those who positively wanted a Federalist solution would have seen it, from their point of view correctly, as a first step towards the 'necessary' acceptance of a Single Currency. (A Single Currency is actually more of a 'sufficient' rather than just a 'necessary' condition for a Federalist state of Europe.)

The second reason for linking the British currency to the Deutschmark was the argument that by so doing Britain would benefit from being inextricably tied to 'sound' German financial policies, especially those aimed at controlling inflation. If inflationary pressures began to mount in Britain there would be no 'soft option' or 'quick fix' available to her in the form of devaluing her way out of trouble.

The idea that the non-German countries of Europe will be better off by linking their currencies and thus their economies – and, indeed, the lives of their citizens – to the Deutschmark provides a large part of the explanation of present establishment thinking and Federalist action throughout Europe. At one point the obsession, especially on the part of the French, was with absorbing Germany (or at least with preventing her from 'getting out of hand'). Now it is with plugging into her perceived economic prowess.

The notion that Germany possesses some magical formula for everlasting material success is deep-rooted and has led to a string of further propositions. It is argued that the 'German model' is suited to all other economies; that its undemocratic features (the prime place given to an unelected Central Bank) are either immaterial or 'a price worth paying'; that it provides the ideal model for a European federal monetary authority; that all the economies of Europe are capable of being synchronised to fit in with the German economic cycle.

These are very important propositions indeed. They form the basis if not of the Federalists' philosophy, then at least of much of the present movement towards a Federalist structure for Europe. In particular, they form the essential backdrop to the Maastricht Treaty of European Union which provides, most importantly, for a Single Currency managed by a single Central Bank. This in turn must lead to a single 'compensatory' and complementary fiscal and taxation authority and thus to the surrender by the nation states of the means for controlling the material well-being and destiny of their citizens.

The view that it is all worth it, in order inextricably to link the destinies of the countries of Europe with that of the Germans, is at least one which is worthy of being tested. It may be as well to start by considering just how successful the German economy has been. Table 2 tells most of the story. It shows that in fact Germany's economic performance, especially in recent years, has not been particularly impressive. Its growth rate has been outstripped for much of the time by that of France and even, in some recent years, by that of the United Kingdom. By 1990 its GDP per head, having of course just absorbed the former East Germany, stood at US$18,970 against the French equivalent of US$19,480. All the Efta countries, including Austria, Switzerland, Finland, Norway and Sweden, have GDP-per-capita levels well above that of Germany and, indeed, any of the other EEC countries with the exception of Luxembourg and Denmark.

The pre-unification figures show that the 'German miracle' was a feature more of the 1950s and 1960s than of later years. Its foundation may have lain as much in the generosity of American post-war assistance as in the wondrous workings of the German financial, industrial and political systems.

It remains true, however, that because of the absolute size of the German economy (now almost the equivalent of that of France and the United Kingdom combined) it is inevitable that she should dominate any European Economic Union, particularly one based upon a Single Currency.

The question now is not whether the other countries of Europe can absorb Germany; it is about the costs and the benefits of latching on to her. For some countries, like

Greece, Portugal and Ireland, no doubt there will continue to be largesse to be gained from her, though for the time being even this is likely to be hard to come by, as Germany piles money into her eastern territory and focuses much of the rest of her financial attentions on her former Communist neighbours. For countries like France and Britain the 'gains' associated with control by an alien system based on a German philosophy and power are more questionable.

Nevertheless, the view has prevailed within the Government, and also within the ranks and higher commands of all the Opposition parties, that Britain's future would be assured by linking herself to the fortunes of another country. This thinking has apparently not been overly concerned with the argument that from that point on it would be not so much what went on in Britain as what happened in Germany which would count most (a phenomenon clearly illustrated by the chart in Appendix 2). Absent apparently has been any appreciation of the unfortunate historical precedent when Britain last linked her economic fortunes to those of another nation.

The decision in 1990 by Britain to join the ERM was, indeed, not the first time this century that she has tried to defend herself from the possible consequences of wrong decisions by her own politicians by linking herself to those made by politicians in another country, through the mechanism of a fixed or managed exchange rate. The previous occasion was in 1925 when, by rejoining the Gold Standard, Britain sought to attach herself to the economy of the United States.

On 15 February 1925, J. M. Keynes wrote of this impending decision:

A Gold Standard means, in practice, nothing but to have the same price level and the same money rates (broadly speaking) as the United States. The whole object is to link rigidly the City and Wall Street. I beg the Chancellor of the Exchequer and the Governor of the Bank of England and the nameless others who settle our destiny in secret to reflect that this may be a dangerous proceeding.

The United States lives in a vast and unceasing crescendo. Wide fluctuations, which spell unemployment and misery for us, are swamped for them in the general upward movement. A country the whole of whose economic activities are expanding, year in, year out, by several per cent per annum cannot avoid, and at the same time can afford, temporary maladjustments. This was our own state during a considerable part of the nineteenth century. Our rate of progress was so great that stability in detail was neither possible nor essential. This is not our state now.[1]

Maynard Keynes's basic point was that the economies of Britain and the United States were very different in terms of their size and state of development. He referred, in particular, to the lack of synchronisation between the economic cycles of the two countries. The parallel between this and the equivalent position today between Britain and Germany is of more than academic interest. Germany now has an economy roughly twice the size of that of Britain. The crucial difference, especially in recent years, between the two countries has been in the timing of their respective economic cycles.

The Gross Domestic Product figures in Table 2 show that Germany's low-growth years (1986–7) were years of fast growth in Britain. It was therefore a time when Germany needed to boost her economy while Britain needed to stabilise hers. In the early nineties the reverse has been the

[1] Quoted from Martin Gilbert, *Winston S. Churchill*, vol. V

case. The fact, however, that Britain linked herself to the German economy through the ERM meant that, far from conducting the opposite policies to Germany's – which it would have been in her real interest to do – she had to follow suit. When German interest rates went down, so did Britain's. When Germany tightened her monetary policy, so did Britain. Far from 'solving' her problems in this way, Britain merely aggravated them. (All this is well illustrated by the chart in Appendix 2.) What is more, given the disparity in size between the two economies, there was never a chance that in this particular waltz British economic interest would be able to take the lead.

Similar considerations worried the Chancellor of the Exchequer, Winston Churchill, in 1925. Agonising about the Gold Standard decision, he wrote to his Controller of Finance at the Treasury, Sir Otto Niemayer:

> The United States has accumulated the greater part of the gold in the world and is suffering from a serious plethora. Are we sure that in trying to establish the Gold Standard we shall not be favouring American interests? Shall we not be making their hoard of gold more valuable than it is at present? Shall we not be relieving them from the consequences of their selfish and extortionate policy? (ibid.)

So one might ask whether by maintaining high interest rates to support the value of the pound against the Deutschmark, the British people were not being required to make untold sacrifices to match German interest rates, whose levels were in part at least caused by that country's need to rebuild her eastern provinces.

Different nations do have different interests. There is nothing 'immoral' or 'moral' about this; it is just a matter of fact. Given the precedent of 1925, it is extraordinary that its lessons have not been learnt: the inadvisability of one country pegging its currency to a more powerful one; the inadvisability, indeed, of that country artificially pegging its currency at all in the face of pressures, speculative and real, which are likely in the fullness of time to force adjustment towards a rate determined by economic forces reflective not of political desire but of relative unit costs between countries.

In both 1925 and 1990 proponents of fixed exchange rates resorted to statements, often unsupported by argument, about their perceived benefits over a properly constituted financial policy for controlling inflation. On each occasion these statements were invariably accompanied by some pretty abusive invective. Montagu Norman, the Governor of the Bank of England in 1925, advised Churchill to brush aside the 'abuse' by the 'ignorant, the gamblers and the antiquated industrialists'. 'The only practical question', he wrote in a letter to Churchill on 2 February 1925, 'is the date', by which he meant the day on which Britain would return to the Gold Standard. The same bombast, one suspects based on the same sense of uncertainty, was to be heard in the early 1990s from those who would have 'discipline' imposed from abroad and unrelated to the needs of the domestic economy. The recent taunts were against the 'quack doctors', 'faint hearts' and 'moaning minnies' who allegedly wished to give up on the fight for low inflation and a stable currency. Nor was it properly explained to the modern British public, any more than it was in 1925, why the 'discipline' could not be imposed direct on the economy without it being necessary to cling to another country's shirt tails to do so.

A partial explanation for this may again be found in the 1925 precedent. On that occasion Lord Bradbury, one of Churchill's two Permanent Secretaries at the Treasury, talked of the Gold Standard being 'knave-proof'. It could not be rigged for political or even more unworthy reasons.

It would prevent our living in a fools' paradise of false prosperity.

The notion that tough political decisions should be taken away from politicians and given, in the case of the Maastricht proposals, to a group of unelected central bankers, is very much in the air today. In this case, it is another way of saying that we wish to be governed neither by elected representatives nor by our own countrymen.

The decision in 1925 turned, however, on a matter which was even more fundamental than making political decisions 'knave-proof'. Churchill summed it up to Keynes after the two men had had a particularly difficult conversation about the matter: 'This isn't entirely an economic decision; it's a political decision.' This does not entirely square with the view that politicians are potentially too 'knavish' to make decisions of any importance, but it was, I suspect, near the mark.

The decision in 1925 to rejoin the Gold Standard had as much to do with wishing to be 'tied up' to the United States of America as was the decision to enter the ERM to do with wishing increasingly to be linked with a centrally governed Europe.

The truth of the matter is that the policy of placing the interests of a managed exchange rate above the real needs of the economy can only be conceived sensibly as part and parcel of a geopolitical strategy to move Britain towards participation in a Single Currency, as required by the Treaty of Maastricht. Its true supporters can only be those who agree with the inevitable Federalist outcome of such a policy.

To those who point to Britain's right, under the Maastricht Treaty on European Union, to choose not to be part of the Single Currency, I recommend a passing glance at a passage in a speech I made in the closing stages of the second reading of the European Communities (Amendment) Bill on 21 May 1992. The House was, as I recollect it, in a rather more highly charged mood than is usual when it discusses European matters. I said – or rather shouted – the following:

> I can imagine, when we have set up the institutions and signed in principle to the treaty, the Whips coming up to me and saying, 'Look here, Spicer, you are talking about this opt-out as if it were a real option. Have you gone completely out of your mind? We have set up the institutions and everybody is joining them. The whole thing is in place. You are out of date. You have got to go along with us. You can't possibly, under these circumstances, start thinking the whole thing out again. We signed it all in 1992. Weren't you there?' The thing will be set in concrete by then.

It has, of course, been a continuous feature of Britain's involvement in Europe that each new step, seen at the time as 'technical', 'consequential', 'of no real account', is later declared to be the point at which the pass was sold.

Whether a Single Currency would be good or bad for Britain is not primarily an economic question, though it would have profound economic effects. Some of these are already apparent following Britain's entry into the ERM: the stoking up of inflation in the mid-1980s and the creation in the 1990s of a million or so extra unemployed, together with thousands of bankruptcies, can properly be ascribed in the main to priority having been given to a managed exchange rate. (And what is a Single Currency if not a permanent system of fixed exchange rates?) It must be hoped that in the 1990s the nature of the modern business cycle is different from what it was in the 1920s and that the long-term devastation caused by Britain's return to the Gold Standard will not be repeated. It will without much doubt remain true, however, that so long as Britain attaches paramount importance to tying her currency in with the Deutschmark and to the other European currencies, her governments will be inhibited from acting in the direct interest of British citizens. This will mean that recovery when it comes is likely to be long-drawn-out and possibly never properly fulfilled.

The real issues surrounding a move towards a Single Currency are above all political. They involve in their essence the consideration of the future of the nation state. This is because, as the Treaty of Maastricht makes plain, a Single Currency is for ever. When a country surrenders its right to issue its own coinage, and does so irrevocably, it loses its sovereignty and thus the basis of its existence as a separate nation state.

This point could not have been made more clearly in July of 1990 by the then Chancellor of the Exchequer, John Major, when in evidence to the Treasury Select Committee of the House of Commons he said:

> The minister responsible for monetary policy should be answerable to the House of Commons . . . By definition a single currency means that this country would no longer have the levers of control over the interest rates or banking policy . . . the Delors proposal for a Stage 3 would involve transfer of sovereignty from the United Kingdom Parliament of a sort neither Government nor Parliament would find themselves able to accept.

The connection between a Single Currency and a single central government is now widely accepted by senior officials and ministers around Europe. Hans Tietmayer, then Deputy President Elect of the Bundesbank, put it this way as early as June 1991: 'A single currency requires a single bank which must be matched by a single government and a single state.'

This has indeed been the thrust of German policy for several years. Chancellor Kohl was very precise on the matter in his Bertelsmann speech on 3 April 1992 calling for a 'United States of Europe'. The Chancellor could not have been more clear as to how, in his view, matters would move forward from the basis of a currency union. These were his words:

> Maastricht has presented us – with clear requirements as to content and time – with the following tasks:
>
> First: the creation by stages of the economic and currency union on the basis of clear and objective criteria.
>
> Second: the formulation of a common foreign policy. Europe over the next few years must be able on all important matters of foreign policy to speak with one voice and, above all, also to act in unison.
>
> Third: the formulation of an independent European security and defence identity.

We have now reached the hub of the matter. The Chancellor of Germany, by far and away, in economic terms, the most powerful country in Europe, has stated that he wishes to see the formation of a federal state of Europe founded on a currency union. What is more, he is confident that the process of transfer of power to the central authority of such a state is now well advanced. We must at last face the question as to whether the time is right to discard the nation state.

Chapter 6

Do We Need the Nation State in Europe?

IT IS hard to imagine that the writer of a book such as this, aiming as he does to address a mainstream readership, would, even two or three years ago, have felt the need seriously to discuss the role and future of the nation state in Europe. It is a measure of how fast and far events have moved that I do so now.

No one suggests, certainly not I, that the nation state has properties which are eternal or that it should attribute to itself values which are timeless. It would, indeed, be foolish and a misreading of history to do so. Nationhood is a relatively modern, mainly European, and at the time of its inception, revolutionary invention. As late as the mid-sixteenth century, Henry VIII acknowledged that when he decreed 'this realm of England is an Empire' it was an act of rebellion directed against the rule of the Church of Rome. The reason why this rebellion was successful was in large measure due to the allegiance which the King was able to command from a people who were already bound together by a common language, system of law and form of government. This sense of common identity was not imposed. Over several centuries it had grown into what was now a natural bond. It is, indeed, the existence of this common interest as part of the natural order – irrespective of what particular regime is in charge – which characterises the nation state. Where it does not exist – as, for instance, in what was Yugoslavia – there is no nation state.

From this sense of shared interest has grown the idea that the citizen should somehow be involved in the process of government. Democracy, at least in its modern institution-alised form, has arisen out of the nation state. In some countries of Europe clearly the democratic institutions are stronger and more deeply rooted than in others; but even where they are weak, the process of political development is conceived of as being one of moving towards a stronger form of democracy and dictatorship is seen as a deviation from the norm.

The question is whether the allegiance and the democratic commitment which goes with it could in the foreseeable future be transferred from the nation state to a federal superstate of Europe. Put like this, the answer is likely to be 'no'. Despite the Euro flag, the Euro anthem and the other paraphernalia of Federalism, no one suggests that there are as yet even the makings of an emotional attachment by the citizens of the European nations to a prospective superstate.

It remains, however, to be considered whether it would be possible to simulate the characteristics of nationhood at federal level by establishing there the appropriate mechanisms. Is it possible, for instance, to create the form of a democratic government out of a federal Europe?

For there to be democracy, there must be accountability by those who govern to those who are governed. In order for this to be the case, at least two conditions must be met. First, the authority being held accountable must genuinely be in authority and, second, those who are holding it accountable should command the sanctions with which to make their wishes effective. They should, in other words, be able to remove the rulers through elections. These are equally crucial conditions for the maintenance of democratic government. One will not do without the other. If, for instance, the national government has been stripped of its ultimate authority, no amount of elections, speeches or appearances on television of politicians will prevent the process from being a twisted perversion of democracy. Members of the national Parliament charged with acting as 'watchdogs' on behalf of the citizens become engaged in acts of total deception as they pass the problems of their constituents up the line to ministers who are no longer in charge.

In order for there to be a democracy there must be a clearly defined source of ultimate power. If this power has been transferred elsewhere, meaningful accountability has ceased to exist. The issue then is whether it can be re-created in the place to which it has moved. In order for this to be possible, the rulers of the new state must be removable through the will of the citizens. Clearly this will not be the case if the rulers are unelected bankers, judges and bureaucrats.

There are some who argue that sovereignty or ultimate authority can be sliced up and shared around. If by this it is meant that there are certain types of decision which can be taken jointly through cooperative arrangements made by different sovereign authorities, there can be little disagreement. In this case the identity of the ultimate authority remains assured. The same is true with arrangements made to delegate authority which can be retrieved at the will of the sovereign government. The essential point, if there is to be proper democratic accountability, is that there must be a clearly defined authority whose judgement and power cannot ultimately be contradicted other than by the citizens themselves through the ballot box. In this sense sovereignty cannot be carved up. Ultimate authority has to exist somewhere.

The problem in Europe is that it is already becoming difficult to decide where ultimately authority does reside. The process of accountability is becoming murky.

The attack on the sovereignty of national governments is coming from at least two directions. I have discussed the impact that moves towards a Single Currency may have, especially if the Maastricht Treaty were to come into force. I now want to consider the other factor: Lord Denning's tidal wave of law arising out of the Treaty of Rome and its various amendments.

In his brilliant pamphlet, *Europe and the Constitution after Maastricht*, produced for the Society of Conservative lawyers, Martin Howe argued that the Community law can already be conceived as being on a higher level than national law:

> The Treaty of Rome requires that its provisions, and many very important regulations and decisions by the Community institutions established under the Treaty, be incorporated as part of the internal laws of all Member States. Thus the Treaty and the subordinate Community legislation are made binding directly upon businesses and private individuals within Member States, and may also be used to challenge the governmental authorities and legislatures of Member States.

The Treaty of Rome indeed differs from other international treaties in this important respect: it requires that its provisions, and those made by amendments to it (such as the Single European Act and the Maastricht Treaty), as well as all the regulations issued by the institutions which it establishes, be incorporated directly into the legal systems of the Member States.

107

This Community law is applied through the courts of the Member States, where it takes precedence over any national law; Martin Howe again:

> A national court which is called upon . . . to apply provisions of Community law is under a duty to give full effect to those provisions, if necessary refusing of its own motion to apply any conflicting provisions of national legislation, even if adopted subsequently, and it is not necessary for the court to request or await a prior setting aside of such provisions by legislative or constitutional means.

In order to provide for such a constitutional amendment, Parliament passed the European Communities Act in 1972, which stated that the requirements arising now or subsequently from the Treaty 'are without further enactment to be given legal effect or used in the United Kingdom' (*European Communities Act*, section 2(1)). The Act goes on to state that any future parliamentary enactment is subject to this new order (ibid., section 2(4)).

While the new order clearly meant that the Community law supplanted existing statute law, the concept that it should likewise override any later Acts of Parliament caused some legal debate, for it seemed to run contrary to the doctrine that no Parliament might bind its successors (Howe, op. cit., p. 13). Community law itself clearly claims to override the constitutional arrangements of a Member State: 'The validity of a Community measure or its effect within a Member State remains unimpaired even if it is alleged that it runs counter to either fundamental rights as formulated by the Constitution of that State or the principles of a national constitutional structure' (*Internationale Handelsgesellschaft* v. *Einfuhr und Vorratsstelle Getreide*).

On these grounds, Acts of Parliament which inadvertently contradict elements of Community law are modified so as to comply with the European Communities Act. The extent to which deliberate Acts of Parliament are able to contradict Community law is a more vexed question, although it found some answer in the case of the Spanish-owned fishing companies in 1991.

Taking advantage of Britain's comparatively liberal laws on the registration of fishing vessels, a number of Spanish fishermen were registering as British companies in order to fish Britain's quota of EEC stocks. The British Government, seeing that this practice clearly violated the spirit of the agreement on fishing quotas which gave some protection to the British fishing industry, passed the Merchant Shipping Act of 1988 restricting British registration of fishing vessels to British individuals and companies.

The Spanish-owned companies which had been involved in 'quota-hopping' challenged the 1988 Act on the grounds that it contradicted Community law. British courts then disapplied the Act; after several appeals, the European Court ruled that this suspension was valid, and the 1988 Act was overruled in 1991.

The legal implications of these events are of the utmost significance. The precedent has now been established that European Community law is invulnerable to deliberate Acts of Parliament, and that British courts are under obligation to disapply those Acts where they conflict with it. The threat which this arrangement poses to the doctrine of parliamentary sovereignty is obvious. There is no protection against this growing accumulation of power.

The precedent is being established that Community law, whether this takes the form of Commission Directives or of judgments by the Court of Justice, overrides national law if the two are in conflict. Lying behind this is the fact that the European Court of Justice has grasped unto itself the role of final arbiter in any dispute between European bodies and national courts in cases where Community law applies.

109

These judgments now stretch far beyond matters of trade between countries – the original *raison d'être* provided by the Treaty of Rome for a separate body of law. The Court's competence has been accepted to cover such matters as, for instance, Sunday trading, working hours, the equality of the sexes and whether or not a road should be built through the English countryside at Twyford Down in Hampshire.

As to whether national governments are still ultimately in charge, the only matter left to be resolved is whether they retain the means to call a halt to the whole process by which law-making is rapidly ceasing to be their responsibility. Is it still feasible for the British Parliament to pass an Act repealing or amending the 1972 European Communities Act which enshrined the Treaty of Rome in British law? What, in particular, remains of the doctrine of the sovereignty of Parliament by which no one Parliament may bind the actions of its successor?

It is significant that these questions are now hotly debated by lawyers. Their answers are no longer definitive and certain. It would seem that the consensus of legal opinion, at least in Britain, is still that the position has not yet been reached where the British Parliament would be constitutionally prohibited from severing or amending Britain's commitment to the Treaty of Rome – though that position is now perilously close.

The process, it would seem, is not yet irrevocable. In this sense sovereignty still rests with the British Parliament. Time is running out, but Parliament can, if it wishes, apparently still draw lines in the sand.

For how much longer will it be possible to maintain this position? For how much longer will it be possible, in theory at least, for Britain to change the basis of her relationship with the EEC? The question is a crucial one. As Martin Howe puts it: 'The existence of an ultimate right of secession is the ultimate touchstone of the continued existence of the sovereignty of the nation state.' The point of no return will certainly be reached if the philosophy and provisions of the Maastricht Treaty and the secular rise of European law join forces.

The key word in Maastricht is 'irrevocable', used in Article 3A in the context of the fixing of exchange rates and the establishment of a Single Currency. The *Oxford Dictionary*'s definition of 'irrevocable' is 'unalterable', 'gone beyond recall'. If Britain finally signs up to the word 'irrevocable', she will have crossed the Rubicon. To have surrendered all power over the issue of her coinage is significant enough, for reasons already argued; to have done so for good must constitute the act of transfer of sovereignty by the British Parliament to another power.

Two proposals have been offered by way of comfort should this be the outcome. The first is that national interests can be guarded by way of intergovernmental agreements made in association with the Treaties. These can take the form of explanatory words of comfort agreed between governments, as for instance discussed at the Birmingham meeting of Heads of Government on 16 October 1992; or they can be formal 'Declarations' appended to the Treaties. An example of this procedure is the Declaration on border controls and immigration which Britain succeeded in appending to the Single European Act.

In neither case are these agreements directly part of the text of the Treaty and therefore of the constitutional law recognised by the Court of Justice. Just as speeches by ministers made in association with the passage of an Act of Parliament are of little or no interest to a judge when he comes to interpret the law, so it is highly unlikely, though the matter has yet fully to be put to the test, that the Court of Justice will take much notice of intergovernmental pronouncements or agreements. All the indications are that all that counts with the Court is the Treaty of Rome and the specific amendments to it.

111

It was to try to shed some further light on this matter that on 2 July 1992, by way of a written question, I asked the Government its view of the legal status of agreements appended to treaties amending the Treaty of Rome. The answer given by Tristan Garel-Jones, a Minister of State at the Foreign and Commonwealth Office, was instructive. It indicated the Government's own recognition of the difference in legal status between Protocols, which are annexes to treaties, and Declarations, which are not. Reference to the law of treaties is, of course, irrelevant in this context, since this is the international law which binds only one Government to another and does not therefore commit a country to a constitutional or legislative change, as does the Treaty of Rome. Hansard of 2 July 1992 reported the interchange between myself and Tristan Garel-Jones as follows:

Mr Michael Spicer: [May I] ask the Secretary of State for Foreign and Commonwealth Affairs if he will list the cases involving the United Kingdom in which there have been adjudications of enforceability of Declarations or agreements appended to international treaties, including EC treaties.

Mr Garel-Jones: In the case of the EC treaties and the treaties amending them there has been a practice of annexing protocols to the treaties and of adopting Declarations in connection with conclusion of the treaties. By Article 239 of the Treaty of Rome, protocols annexed to the treaty form an integral part of it. They are, therefore, enforceable in exactly the same way as treaty provisions. A case involving the United Kingdom where this was done is *Lord Bruce of Donington* v. *Aspden*, case 208/80, applying the Protocol on privileges and immunities of the European Communities. Conference Declarations do not form an integral part of the treaty to which they relate, but, in accordance with the law of treaties, they are part of the context of the treaty for the purpose of its interpretation. I am aware of no decision of the European Court of Justice in which conference Declarations of this kind have been pronounced upon.

An important implication of this, in the context of attempts which may be made to encourage Denmark to change her mind, is that assurances and comforting words which are not directly part of the Treaty are unlikely to be worth the paper they are written on, or the microphone they are spoken from, so far as the emerging European law is concerned.

The second idea for reducing the impact of the legal onrush towards a Federalist future has been the concept of 'subsidiarity'. The word has the strength and the weakness that no one quite knows what it means. This lack of clarity in the meaning of subsidiarity is in one sense rather surprising. The search for a proper definition has certainly been on in the House of Commons for several years. My parliamentary colleague, the Member for Ludlow, Christopher Gill, has been leading the chase. As early as 4 April 1990 there was the following exchange between him and Francis Maude, then Minister of State at the Foreign and Commonwealth Office:

Mr Gill: [May I] ask the Secretary of State for Foreign and Commonwealth Affairs what assurances he has sought that the policy of subsidiarity would operate to the benefit of the United Kingdom.

Mr Maude: We support the principle of subsidiarity as an important way of avoiding unnecessary legislation at Community level. There is widespread support for the principle across the Community, and we believe that it should be rigorously applied in practice.

Mr Gill: Given the reluctance of large organisations and bureaucracies to devolve powers to the lower orders, does my hon. Friend consider that for the principle of subsidiarity to be acceptable it will be necessary for a full and detailed prospectus to be issued showing what powers will be devolved to the national Parliaments?

Mr Maude: I am not sure that I regard the nation states of Europe as the lower orders. I accept my hon. Friend's point that it is important that there should be the maximum leaving of powers to the nation states, the Member States of the Community. On the desirability or otherwise of a comprehensive list of what should be done at each level, the best way to proceed is for there to be a presumption, effectively, that matters are best dealt with at national level unless it can be shown that that is better done at Community level. That is the principle of subsidiarity, which has been widely subscribed to by political leaders across the European Community. Our concern is that the words are not yet matched by deeds. It is important that they should be.

This was followed on 13 June 1992 by the following question and answer between Gill and the Foreign Secretary:

Mr Gill: With regard to subsidiarity, my right hon. Friend will be aware of the necessity to protect the best features of our national and local democracy. What assurance can he give the House that that will amount to more than crumbs from the European Commission's table?

Mr Hurd: I listened to my hon. Friend's particularly interesting speech on that theme on Monday, and I commend it to the House. The powers of the European Community are not vested in the Community and then, as it were, the Community lets us have some crumbs from the table. It is the other way round. In the Treaty of Rome, the Treaty of Accession and the Single European Act, this country, this Government and this Parliament have given certain clearly defined powers to the Community. Therefore, those powers cannot be increased without the same process and amendment of the treaties.

Sadly, as I shall explain, the facts do not bear out the interpretation given to them by the Foreign Secretary.

The inclusion of 'subsidiarity' in the Maastricht Treaty on European Union has been presented as a great victory for those who wanted to see the centralising, Federalist and irrevocable proposals of the Treaty given some sort of counterbalance for the rights of the nation state. Subsidiarity does no such thing. Indeed, it merely reinforces the Federalist tendency.

The relevant words of Article 3B of the Treaty in this context are: 'Any action by the Community shall not go beyond what is necessary to achieve the objectives of the Treaty.'

The essential question, of course, is that of who is to determine 'what is necessary to achieve the objectives of the Treaty'.

There can be no doubt as to the answer. Matters of dispute on Community competence are the preserve of the Court of Justice. The perceived role of the Court and of the Commission as the twin guardians of the Treaty will be sufficient in practice to ensure that the Commission will determine the limits of its own field of competence so far as

Article 3B and subsidiarity are concerned. Indeed, that is precisely what is happening. It is the Commission, for example, which quite overtly decided not to intervene in the decision to build a road through Twyford Down in Hampshire, but which apparently will continue to challenge the plans for an East London river crossing at Oxleas Wood, as well as proposals by British Petroleum for a gas terminal at Falkirk. What any of these matters have to do with intercountry trade or a single market in Europe is not readily apparent.

The notion of subsidiarity as being a fail-safe device against the destruction of national powers by the centralising force of Brussels is a misleading one. In fact, it is the reverse of that. The very concept assumes the existence of a higher power than that of the nation state. Because of the way in which it is proposed to incorporate 'subsidiarity' into the European constitution, it will actually augment the powers of the Federalist institutions, which will be left with the essential decisions about how it is to be defined and applied. Far from acting as a buffer against Federalism, it will actually assist it.

The fact is that the pace towards a federal Europe is quickening and there is now very little, save the Danes and the British Parliament, which lies in its way.

So it is no longer such a hypothetical question to ask, if the nation state were to be abolished (at least in the sense that it was no longer governed by a sovereign government directly accountable for its actions to the people), would a new form of democracy, perhaps more potent than that offered by the nation state, rise from the ashes?

It would mean at the very least, firmly subjugating the Commission to an elected authority. There is no sign at all of this or anything like it happening. Indeed, one of the features of the Federalist movement appears to be a desire to abolish decision-making by politicians or by elected representatives. This, as has been said, is particularly true of the moves to set up an unaccountable Central Bank. It is also true of the proposals to reduce the powers of the Council of Ministers.

Another approach to democratising the federal state of Europe would be one which relied upon strengthening the European Parliament.

I have already put forward my view that in the foreseeable future there is unlikely to be a sufficiency of common purpose or tradition to create out of a federal Parliament the necessary cohesion for it to control, or even to have much influence over, the unelected central bodies, especially the Commission and the Court of Justice. The idea is simply not credible to me that the British people will be able to exert their will through a European Parliament on such matters as, for instance, how many people from beyond their shores will be able to settle here or whether taxes should be lowered – thus halting, perhaps, some road-building programme in Greece – or whether Britain should continue to maintain her close links across the Atlantic.

Of course, British Members of the European Parliament if they so wished could make their points and their views known. That is not the issue. The question is whether there would be a sufficient merging of interest between, for instance, the anti-American stance of the French, the Central European posture of the Germans, the Mediterranean outlook of the Greeks and the mercantile perspective of the British for there to be a cohesive common position sufficient to enable the Parliament to hold the executive bodies accountable. I do not think so. But even if the answer is merely uncertain, the decisions will continue to be left to the unelected institutions, who will plough their course without significant interference. Far from increasing the democratic accountability provided at present – no one says perfectly – by the nation state, we will have all but obliterated it. This is an especially serious prospect for Britain, whose deeply rooted democratic institutions remain the envy

117

of many of the other countries of the EEC. Indeed, it may well be that the weakness in their democratic institutions explains why some of the Member States show no great concern about the threat to democracy posed by the present moves towards a federal state of Europe.

The acid test of whether there is a continuing role for the nation state remains whether the citizens of Britain, for instance, would wish or feel able to transfer their allegiance to a government in Brussels. I do not believe they would. Virtually everything else follows from this proposition.

The question is whether the Treaty of Maastricht would make such a transfer of allegiance imperative. The time has come to look at the Treaty of European Union and the philosophy which lies behind it in a little more detail.

Chapter 7

Maastricht: The Federalist Agenda

D EPENDING ON one's view of the future, the Treaty on European Union is either the high-water mark or the latest bench-mark of European Federalism. In either case, its initialling at Maastricht by Heads of Government on 10 December 1991 was an event of immense importance. Its contents certainly merit much closer attention than on the whole has been made possible for the general public around Europe.

The Treaty was formally signed by representatives of the Governments of the Twelve on 7 February 1992, and was set to come into force on 1 January 1993 following parliamentary ratification by each of the Member States 'or, failing that, on the first day of the month following the deposit of the instrument of ratification by the last signatory State to take this step' (Article R).

The Treaty comprises amendments to the Treaty of Rome as well as extensive new provisions. It is divided into seven sections, called Titles.

Title I establishes the European Union as a formal entity.

Title II makes considerable amendments to the Treaty

establishing the EEC (which it renames as the European Community).

Title III makes the same institutional alterations to the European Coal and Steel Community as does Title II to the EEC.

Title IV makes these alterations to the European Atomic Energy Community.

Title V provides for a Common Foreign and Security policy.

Title VI provides for harmonisation in the fields of Justice and Home Affairs.

Title VII contains various miscellaneous 'Final Provisions'.

Under the terms of the Treaty, the parties 'establish among themselves a European Union, hereinafter called "the Union"'. The stated objectives of this Union include 'to assert its identity on the international scene', 'to develop close cooperation on justice and home affairs' and to 'maintain in full and build upon the *acquis communautaire*' (i.e. the process by which EEC authority is irreversibly entrenched in any area in which it has once legislated – a principle hitherto unrecognised in law). Article F(3) states: 'The Union shall provide itself with the means necessary to attain its objectives and carry through its policies.'

Citizenship of the Union is established, with the nationals of every Member State 'subject to the duties imposed thereby'.

The Treaty creates a European Central Bank, and provides for the establishment of a Single Currency in three stages (a special Protocol allows the United Kingdom to opt out of stage three of this process, but not stages one and two). In the meantime, Member States are required to regard their economic policies as 'a matter of common concern', and to obey 'broad guidelines of the economic policies of the Member States and the Community'. They are also required to 'avoid excessive Government deficits', and may eventually be fined for non-compliance.

Community authority is greatly extended, both in existing areas and in new ones, including social policy, education and training, health, consumer protection, the environment, industry and culture. A Committee of the Regions is set up, with *carte blanche* to decide upon its procedures and its programmes, and the scope for 'Cohesion' transfer payments is widened.

Finally, a conference is scheduled for 1996 to revise and extend the terms of the Treaty.

It is fair to point out that many of the apparently new areas in which Community jurisdiction is established had already been anticipated by, or incorporated in, previous EEC legislation. The EEC does not require new intergovernmental conferences or fresh treaties in order to extend many of its areas of competence. Articles 100 and 235 of the Treaty of Rome provide a mechanism whereby the amassment of power by the Community may be carried on as a continuous process. Just as the Single European Act gave formal recognition to several existing developments in such areas as the environment, so does the Treaty on European Union put an official stamp on the *de facto* extension of Community powers in such fields as public health, consumer protection and tourism.

This notwithstanding, the Treaty on European Union differs from previous Community treaties in its scope and in its ambition. Whereas the Treaty of Rome and the Single European Act both appeared to be at least chiefly concerned with trade and economic cooperation, the Treaty on European Union is involved with almost every policy with which a national government could concern itself. There has until now been a degree of ambiguity in the presentation of the goal of political union. Such ambiguity is dispersed by the Maastricht Treaty.

British Government spokesmen have suggested from time to time that the Treaty on European Union represents a reversal of the process of centralisation within the Community. One reason given for this is that a distinction is created within the Treaty between those matters (under Titles II, III and IV) which, as amendments to the Treaty of Rome, are changes to the law of the land, and those aspects (Titles I, V, VI and VII) which concern the new entity of the European Union and are the subject of intergovernmental agreement and which do not therefore in a strict sense affect British law (the stated reason why only Titles II, III and IV are subject to parliamentary ratification).

The distinction has been more in the minds of the negotiators (especially the British negotiators) than it has been a reality or, more important, likely to be given much credence by the Court of Justice if and when it comes to adjudicate on the basis of the Treaty.

First, there exists a considerable degree of overlap between the various titles. The creation of Union citizenship is provided for in Title II as an amendment to the Treaty of Rome – not in the Titles concerned with intergovernmental agreements. European citizenship is therefore subject to the jurisdiction of the European Court, belying the notion that the Union is separate from the Community. Second, Titles V and VI make it explicitly clear that just as with other aspects of Community life, the institutions of the EEC, in particular the Commission, are to be fully involved in 'Union' foreign and home policy. Third, the formal recognition of the *acquis communautaire*, provided for under Title I, in effect applies the notion of irreversible embracement by EEC institutions to the intergovernmental agreements.

It is therefore clear that the distinction between the different 'pillars' of the Maastricht Treaty is at best intended to be temporary and at worst is wholly meaningless. If the negotiators of the Treaty had truly intended intergovernmental cooperation to be means by which the Community would develop into a Union, they would not have involved

EEC institutions directly in this process. They would not have blurred the distinction between the Union and the Community. The arrangements proposed in Maastricht can only lead to the eventual fusion of the various pillars.

There was some hope at the time of the Maastricht negotiations that the centralising tendencies of the European Community would be checked by the 'principle of subsidiarity'. I discussed in the previous chapter some of the political questions raised by subsidiarity; now let me briefly consider one or two legal matters it raises.

The subsidiarity principle is stated in a new Article 3B which reads:

> In areas which do not fall within its exclusive competence, the Community shall take action, in accordance with the principle of subsidiarity, only if and in so far as the objectives of the proposed action cannot be sufficiently achieved by the Member States and can therefore, by reason of the scale or effects of the proposed action, be better achieved by the Community.

This Article does not affirm or imply the converse: that actions which can be sufficiently achieved by Member States should be performed by them.

Proposals might be made for action at European Community level which do not fall within the Community's exclusive competence and which certain Member States regard as undesirable or unnecessary. In such a case, it is clear that if left to the Member States, the Community-wide action would not take place. This could be interpreted with reference to Article 3B, 'the objectives of the proposed action cannot be . . . achieved by the Member States' and the principle of subsidiarity would thus provide no obstacle to the Community's action. In the words of Leolin Price, QC:

'All that is needed in any particular matter is to show that some individual Member State will not take government action at Member State level to achieve what is proposed. That will establish the lawfulness of governmental action by the Community to achieve what is proposed.'

There is no proper definition of the subsidiarity principle in the text of the Maastricht Treaty, and nor does the word have any general legal meaning. In the absence of any formal legal constraint upon European Community actions, the question of whether any given circumstances invalidate Community action is left solely to the European Court at Luxembourg.

The Maastricht Treaty represents more than a consolidation of the process of centralisation in the EEC. If ratified, it would signal a massive official expansion of Community competence into non-economic areas.

Let us now briefly examine some of the areas into which the scope of EEC authority is extended for the first time.

FOREIGN AND SECURITY POLICY

The provisions for a common foreign and security policy come in Title V of the Maastricht Treaty. Title V, being ostensibly concerned with intergovernmental agreement, is among those parts of the Treaty which are not available for parliamentary debate or for a vote in Parliament.

Article J.1 of that Title declares: 'The Union and its Member States shall define and implement a common foreign and security policy, governed by the provisions of this Title and covering all areas of foreign and security policy.' It goes on to define the objective of this policy as safeguarding 'the common values, fundamental interests and independence of the Union'. And Article J.4 says: 'The common foreign and security policy shall include all questions related to the security of the Union, including the

eventual framing of a common defence policy.'
Moreover:

> The Member States shall support the Union's external
> and security policy actively and unreservedly in a
> spirit of loyalty and mutual solidarity. They shall
> refrain from any action which is contrary to the inter-
> ests of the Union or likely to impair its effectiveness as
> a cohesive force in international relations. The Coun-
> cil shall ensure that these principles are complied
> with.

This last sentence may appear to safeguard the Member
States' authority, at least in the field of applying the foreign
policy of the Union. It does not, however, equate with a
national right of veto. Lest there be any doubts about this,
consider the Maastricht Declaration on Voting in the Field
of the Common Foreign and Security Policy: 'The Conference agrees that, with regard to Council decisions requiring
unanimity, Member States will, to the extent possible, avoid
preventing a unanimous decision where a qualified majority exists in favour of that decision.'

Interestingly, this was not included in the main section of
the Treaty dealing with foreign and security policy but was
tacked innocuously on to the end. It amounts to an agreement by Member States not to employ their veto to prevent
a majority decision, and effectively represents a reversal of
the Luxembourg Compromise. Under the terms of the
Compromise, Member States were supposedly given the
right to veto decisions affecting their vital national interests; under the terms of this Maastricht Declaration they
effectively renounce that right, thus giving to foreign policy
at the outset the same status as that acquired by other areas
of policy where the Compromise has gradually been eroded
over many years.

Finally: 'The Commission shall be fully associated with the work carried out in the common foreign and security field' (Article J.9).

The formal extension of EEC competence into the field of defence and foreign affairs is a profound and radical change in the nature of the Community and must raise the question: why now?

For four decades after the signing of the Treaty of Paris, all the Member States of the EEC faced a common menace from the aggressive and expansionist Warsaw Pact. It was fear of the Soviet military threat which led many US administrations to work for the political unification of Europe – a process in many ways inimical to their own interests – and to urge the United Kingdom to play her part. The wish to defend European freedom and democracy was central to Britain's attitude towards the EEC and, as I have said, comprised one of the chief arguments which I deployed when campaigning for a 'Yes' vote in 1975.

In August 1991, the shadow of Communist imperialism was finally lifted from Europe; in December of that year, the EEC Heads of Government negotiated the Maastricht Treaty. Thus, at the very moment when the common menace receded, the Twelve committed themselves to a common defence policy. In the absence of any obvious threat to their collective security, it is impossible to avoid asking what made this step so necessary.

With the exception of the Irish Republic, each of the Member States of the EEC is also a member of Nato, as are the United States, Canada, Iceland, Norway and Turkey. The North Atlantic Treaty defines an attack upon any of its signatories as an attack on all members. Nato is served by an integrated military command structure, from which France withdrew in 1965 as the result of General de Gaulle's hostility to 'Anglo-Saxon domination', although she remains a signatory to the Treaty and is bound by its terms. As a force for maintaining peace and preserving freedom,

Nato has been the most successful military alliance in history.

Title V of the Maastricht Treaty stipulates that the Common Foreign and Security Policy 'shall respect the obligations of certain Member States under the North Atlantic Treaty'; but this does not explain why a new structure is necessary at all. The argument that the European Union should form its own defence system alongside Nato suggests that the Member States are not capable of integrating their defences sufficiently through existing Nato structures. If the Union must have a security structure of its own, it necessarily follows that it has needs which are not covered by Nato and interests which go beyond the mutual defence guaranteed by the North Atlantic Treaty.

The only practical argument advanced by the supporters of the common European security policy is based upon the fact of the withdrawal of US troops from Western Europe. This argument takes one of two forms depending upon the outlook of its proponent: either it is said that Europe must look to her own defence as a consequence of the American disengagement; alternatively it is argued that Europe ought in principle to defend herself, so as to speed the departure of the US troops and be free of American 'domination'.

Setting aside the question of whom Europe must defend herself against, each of these points of view fails to take account of one critical fact: the military structures of Nato, which have proved their worth over forty years, will still be in place regardless of any diminution of the American presence in Europe. Europe is capable of maintaining an effective common security within those structures, and with the additional guarantee of US and Canadian assistance in the event of war. The creation of a security system outside Nato in no way improves upon the security provided by existing Nato military structures.

A European Common Foreign and Security Policy is thus unrelated to any military assessment of Europe's defence needs. It reflects instead a brand of thinking which is prepared to pay a military price in terms of diminished security, in return for the political goal of Europe as 'a cohesive force in international relations'.

Peter Schmidt of the Stiftung Wissenschaft Politik at Ebenhausen, a leading expert on European defence and security issues, has identified the formulation of a Common Foreign and Security Policy as the product of a 'top-down approach' which 'regards the political union of Western Europe within the framework of the EC as an end in itself', rather than of a 'functional or horizontal approach' which 'asks in a practical way which defence functions can and should be handled in a Western European framework, which ones can remain attached to existing defence arrangements – above all that means Nato – and which ones can stay at the disposal of nation states'.

This is perhaps the right moment to lay to rest the myth that the loss of sovereignty involved in membership of the EEC is no different from that involved in membership of any international organisation (Nato is the example most often quoted). The difference is real and profound. Nato is an association of independent states whose interests coincide to the extent that they have chosen to adopt a common structure within which to cooperate. This structure can neither impose law upon its members nor force one of them to adopt a policy with which it disagrees. Nato is controlled by the governments of its member nations, not by a Nato Commission or a Nato Parliament. The extent to which cooperation and, indeed, common policies exist among Nato members is testimony to what can be achieved by sovereign states acting together in amity.

In assessing the likely effectiveness of the Common Foreign and Security Policy, it is important to look at the examples of joint European Community foreign-policy ventures to date. The record is instructive. There have been two great international crises since the collapse of Communism in Eastern Europe: the Gulf War and the disintegration of Yugoslavia. Both events revealed not only deep divisions among Member States, but also fundamentally flawed policies.

The Gulf War witnessed an extraordinary lack of resolve across the EEC. Germany interpreted her constitution as forbidding her to participate in the military operation, and Belgium refused to sell ammunition to the British army. There can be little doubt that under the terms of the Common Foreign and Security Policy, there would have been no European response to Saddam Hussein's aggression.

The EEC's response to the disintegration of Yugoslavia is an equally important indication of what might be expected from the Common Foreign and Security Policy. The Community began by taking the line that federations were clearly a more advanced form of government than nation states: it refused to countenance any challenge to 'the integrity of Yugoslavia' and, under the Presidency of Luxembourg, made clear to the Slovenes that small countries were not viable in the new Europe. The EEC further stated that the continuation of its economic support was contingent upon the unity of Yugoslavia, and that the constituent Yugoslav republics would be denied individual entry into the Community. Thus encouraged, the Serbs continued their expansion into Croatia, where the EEC's refusal to recognise Croatian independence gave them the status of a legitimate federal army. When the Community belatedly recognised the *de facto* independence of the Yugoslav republics, it was acting too late for its recognition to have any effect beyond aggravating the fighting. Since then, EEC policy has been characterised by inactivity, timidity, and a total failure to halt the fighting, the atrocities or the refugee crisis.

These problems are unsurprising when one considers the diversity of the national interests of the Member States:

129

Denmark's quasi-neutrality, Germany's delicate constitutional problems, France's dislike of fighting alongside the United States, Britain's willingness to do so. Of the resolutions in the UN General Assembly requiring a vote, EEC consensus was achieved in only 33 per cent of cases in 1990 and 40 per cent in 1991. Given this reality, a Common Foreign and Security Policy can only be expected to reflect the lowest common denominator, the position which least offends.

The history of the European Fighter Aircraft project is in many ways a microcosm of the proposed Common Foreign and Security Policy. Motivated by rather more than just military considerations, the EFA was an exercise in European unity, and was governed by the need to give a 'fair share' of the contracts to each of the participating countries. The French refused to take part in the project because Dassault was not to receive the largest proportion of the contracts and, in June 1992, Germany decided that, since the threat from the Warsaw Pact was gone and she was unlikely to participate in out-of-area conflicts, she had no more use for the aircraft. Britain, which saw the possibility of having to act in out-of-area conflicts and thus still needed an effective fighter aircraft, was left with the decision as to whether or not to proceed with the project unilaterally.

The enlargement of the EEC to include Sweden, Finland, Austria and Switzerland can only have the effect of lowering the common denominator still further, and of weakening the position of those states which still have national interests to pursue in the world. It might have been thought that the arrival of so many neutral countries would render any Common Security Policy impossible, but the Community institutions are alert to this 'danger', and have stated that they will be rigorous in their application of the *acquis* to new members.

On 31 July 1992, the Commission declared: 'Specific and binding assurances from Sweden should be sought with regard to her political commitments and legal capacity to fulfil the obligations . . . (on) the eventual framing of a common defence policy.'

The Swedish Prime Minister, Carl Bildt, justly complained that 'membership has unspecified potential obligations', and that Sweden thus could not be expected to make binding assurances that she would participate in a common defence policy which has not yet been defined. Any European Common Foreign and Security Policy which includes Swedish and other neutral interests must be less effective even than that which can be expected to emerge from the current unsatisfactory record of EEC action in foreign affairs.

Mark Almond of the Institute for European Defence and Strategic Studies has pointed out that

> it ought to be possible for partners to disagree on specifics while remaining allied in general terms and often working together in many fields. All agreeing to be wrong or at best ineffective is not going to make the voice of Europe louder in the councils of the world. The danger is that all Twelve risk making themselves equally irrelevant, even when crises erupt on their own doorstep.

This being so, one is again forced to ask why effective cooperation is to be sacrificed to the principle of an ineffective, if unanimous, common policy. If the Member States of the EEC were concerned chiefly with their security and with an effective system of collective military strength, they would work through the structures of Nato, whose durability and success are well proven. What the Common Foreign and Security Policy represents is not a realistic and objective response to Europe's security needs, but the establishment of a unified European foreign policy in

131

principle because it is felt that the European Union, as an 'independent' entity, ought to be served by such a policy. Just as in their trade policy the Federalists are prepared to sacrifice the Member States' economic prosperity for the political goal of a United Europe, so does the establishment of a Common Foreign and Security Policy sacrifice their military and strategic needs to that same political end.

The Franco-German army corps encapsulates this philosophy in miniature. Using wholly incompatible weapons systems and riven by language difficulties, the troops lack the capacity to fight as coordinated units. While widely recognised as militarily irrelevant, the Franco-German brigades are being enlarged as a successful symbol of European cooperation. As does the whole concept of the Common Foreign and Security Policy, they represent a way of thinking which sees military capability as relatively unimportant beside the dream of a powerful and independent European Union, speaking with one voice and free from American interference.

The Maastricht Treaty is a specific and conscious step in the direction of Euro-nationalism as an end in itself. Title V rules out for ever a return to the alternative: a degree of foreign-policy alignment reflecting the reality of diverging national interests and a European Community whose members express their friendship and community of interests by cooperating through the most effective available means. If Title V were taken to its logical conclusions, one would surely be entitled to speculate as to whether the nations of Europe would continue to be permitted their own separate seats on the international bodies and in the United Nations.

HOME AFFAIRS AND IMMIGRATION

Title VI of the Maastricht Treaty sets out provisions on

cooperation in the fields of justice and home affairs. Like Title V on foreign and security policy, being 'intergovernmental' it may be ratified by the Government without Parliamentary assent, and is not to be debated in Parliament.

The following are defined as matters of common interest 'for the purposes of achieving the objectives of the Union':

1. Asylum policy;
2. Rules governing the crossing by persons of the external borders of the Member States and the exercise of controls thereon;
3. Immigration policy and policy regarding nationals of third countries:
   (a) conditions of entry and movement by nationals of third countries on the territory of Member States;
   (b) conditions of residence by nationals of third countries on the territory of Member States, including family reunion and access to employment;
   (c) combating unauthorised immigration, residence and work by nationals of third countries on the territory of Member States;
4. Combating drug addiction in so far as this is not covered by 7 to 9;
5. Combating fraud on an international scale in so far as this is not covered by 7 to 9;
6. Judicial cooperation in civil matters;
7. Judicial cooperation in criminal matters;
8. Customs cooperation;
9. Police cooperation for the purposes of preventing and combating terrorism, unlawful drug trafficking and other serious forms of international crime, including if necessary certain aspects of

133

customs cooperation, in connection with the organisation of a Union-wide system for exchanging information within a European Police Office (Europol) (Article K.1)

The Council 'may decide that measures implementing joint action are to be adopted by a qualified majority' (Article K.3 2(b)). Also, 'The Commission shall be fully associated with the work in the areas referred to in this Title' (Article K.4 2).

These provisions bring huge new areas under the competence of the institutions of the European Community.

The establishment of a European Police Office (Europol) has been condemned by Interpol as unnecessary and likely to lead to confusion. Its proposed creation is another indication of an attitude in the Community of seeking integration for its own sake. If the European Union is to become a form of national state, it follows that it must have its own police force, just as it must have its own army. The fact that existing structures of policing (or defence) are more effective than what is proposed is less important than the principle that such matters should be the preserve of a united European Government. It is this thinking which has created Title VI of the Maastricht Treaty as the beginning of a process by which responsibility for justice and home affairs is transferred from the jurisdiction of the Member States to that of the European Union.

CULTURE

The 1992 Olympic Games at Barcelona witnessed an extraordinary promotional offensive by the European Economic Community. Blue-and-gold European flags surrounded the stadium, Beethoven's Ninth Symphony (adopted as the European anthem) was played at the opening and closing ceremonies, and the entire arena was at one stage lit up in EEC colours. The cost of these activities was met by EEC taxpayers, and came from the 10,850,000 ECUs sanctioned by M. Jacques Delors as that year's budget for 'the promotion of Europe's cultural identity' (see Adam Breeze, *Culture Vultures*, IFF, 1992).

What occurred none the less fell well short of the Community's original proposals. It was only a dispute over finance with the Olympic authorities which prevented the EEC from enacting a programme in which the athletes of every Member State would have competed in European Community uniforms, mounted the podium to the strains of Beethoven's Ninth in place of their own anthems, and totted up a European total of medals.

These plans came from the Commission's Cultural Directorate, DG-X. The current 'Commissioner with Responsibility for Audio-Visual and Cultural Affairs, Information and Communication and Citizens' Europe' is Jean Dodelinger of Luxembourg. DG-X is motivated by a feeling that European society must be protected from 'American cultural imperialism' and 'Japanese technological domination'. Thus, for example, in response to the 'threat' posed by the American satellite news channel CNN, M. Dodelinger decided to create a European challenge: Euronews. Euronews is to transmit across Europe in English, French, German, Italian and Spanish, paid for wholly by subsidies from the Community budget.

DG-X has at its disposal media subsidies worth 165 million ECUs to be used by 1995.

As with EEC trade and agriculture policies, subsidies are supplemented by protectionism. In 1991, the Commission issued a Directive entitled *Broadcasting Without Frontiers* under the terms of which 'a percentage of programming time must be reserved for programmes of Community origin'. Indeed, 'a majority of drama, documentaries and educational programmes' should be of EEC origin, and a percentage of every television company's budget must be allocated to 'Community works created by independent producers' (the proportion, initially to be 5 per cent, will rise to 10 per cent).

All of this was begun before any official extension of EEC authority into the field of culture. The formal extension would exist if Article 37 of the Treaty on European Union were ratified. This states: 'The Community shall contribute to the flowering of the cultures of the Member States.' Specifically:

> Action by the Community shall be aimed at encouraging cooperation between Member States and, if necessary, supporting and implementing their action in the following areas:
> – improvement of the knowledge and dissemination of the culture and history of the European peoples;
> – conservation and safeguarding of cultural heritage of European significance;
> – non-commercial cultural exchanges;
> – artistic and literary creation, including in the audiovisual sector.

The field of action granted to the Community in culture is thus a wide one. It is not yet clear exactly how it would expand in this area, but the steps it has already taken are illuminating.

As with defence and with home affairs, the cultural policy of the Community demonstrates a willingness to sacrifice quality and effectiveness to the principle of integration as a goal in itself. The current TV Euro-soap *Rivierra* is screened across the EEC from Belgium to Italy. It has entered the record books as the most expensive and least popular programme of its kind: the ratio of the money invested in its making to the number of its viewers is the worst in the history of television. Britain decided not to screen the series, and was widely condemned by the European media for her typically *non-communautaire* attitude. *Rivierra* demonstrates the inherent difficulty of devising a cultural programme which embraces Europeans from Samos to Stornaway.

Article 37 is among the less hotly debated parts of the Treaty on European Union, but it is vitally important in terms of what it represents. The Treaty brings about the formal transformation of what has hitherto been an Economic Community into a Union which is mandated to act in many areas on behalf of its own citizens, and to claim their allegiance. These citizens will be served by instruments of Government at Union level, which are intended eventually to be made democratically accountable. For such a system to function, there has to be a sense of European identity: no citizen of the Union will abide by laws and policies made by institutions which he does not feel to be his own. The Commission and the European Parliament have conducted regular opinion polls over many years to monitor the development of such an identity, but it is still only felt by a small minority of Europeans. The legitimisation in the Maastricht Treaty of the EEC's attempt to promote this identity represents an acknowledgement of the ultimate goal which inspired it. It is why the Commission has accurately described the Maastricht Treaty as an attempt to construct Europe 'on a unitary base'.

Consider what are the constituent elements of a sovereign national state: citizenship, a parliament, a currency, a legal system and judiciary, an independent foreign policy and a diplomatic service, as well as outward symbols such as a passport, a sports team, a national anthem and a flag. The Treaty on European Union lays the foundations for a new state which is to incorporate each of these things. Every British Government department, without exception, will have an equivalent policy-making body at European Union level.

The enshrinement of the principle of the *acquis communautaire*, and the pledge to enlarge upon it, would remove for ever the possibility that the Community might develop in different directions. Articles B and N define the Treaty as the first of a series, the beginning of a process. The Maastricht Treaty thus represents the moment at which all the Federalist tendencies which have been present during four decades of integration emerged and, if ratified, were legally sanctioned. The agenda spelt out by the Treaty on European Union would lead to the eventual transformation of the Community into a single unitary state.

Two misconceptions about the Treaty of Maastricht have been allowed to gain currency. The first is that its signing constituted a reversal of the process towards a federal state of Europe. The second is that there is no alternative to proceeding with its ratification.

I hope that the reader will feel that I have satisfactorily dealt with the first. For the rest of the book I turn to the second and in particular to what lies behind the mounting opposition to the Treaty, away from the fug and the isolation of Cabinet rooms, palaces and Chancelleries.

Chapter 8

The Effect of a Wider Europe

U NTIL VERY recently there has been thought – certainly in Brussels and Strasbourg – to be an inevitability about the eventual federal goal of Western Europe, the *finalité politique*. All of a sudden this certainty is being called into question by dramatic changes in public opinion, and also by new pressures greatly to expand the EEC.

The process towards European integration is generally acknowledged to have begun with the declaration by Robert Schuman, on 9 May 1950, which led to the establishment of the European Coal and Steel Community on 18 April 1951.

Member States at this time were Belgium, France, the Federal Republic of Germany, Italy, Luxembourg and the Netherlands. Meeting at Messina in 1955, representatives of the Governments of these countries agreed to extend the integration of their coal and steel industries to the whole of their economies, and the EEC and Euratom were created in 1957. Membership of the three European Communities was, and has remained, identical, and it was at this time

139

that the Member States became known as 'the Six'.

The first moves towards enlarging the Community came during 1961 and 1962 with the applications of Britain, Denmark, Ireland and Norway.

These applications were vetoed at the time by de Gaulle and his allies, and this veto was upheld in 1967 at the time of their second application. Finally, these countries made considerable concessions to the policies and institutions of the EEC and the Governments of the Six, and were allowed to join in 1972 following permission granted by the French people in a referendum, and with membership subject to parliamentary assent in each of the applicant states. This was granted in the United Kingdom with a majority of eight votes. In the other three countries, popular assent was also required: the Irish and Danish referendums registered 'Yes' votes, while Norway voted 'No'.

The second enlargement of the EEC was that which embraced the newly democratic states of southern Europe. Once again, negotiations were prolonged. Greece applied for membership in 1975 and finally became a Member State on 1 January 1981. Spain and Portugal applied in 1977 and were not admitted until 1986.

Meanwhile, in a little-known episode of the Community's history, Greenland in 1984, following unanimous agreement among the Member States, became the only state to be allowed to withdraw from the EEC; in doing so, it reduced the EEC's land surface area by half. The issue of what might occur if the secession of a Member State were opposed by one or more of the others has never yet arisen.

Both expansions of the European Economic Community led to the central institutions of the Community arguing successfully that, for the enlargement to function, they must be given more powers and the Community's political union must be strengthened. The admission of Britain, Denmark and Ireland led to the setting up of an effective system of Community 'own resources', independent from the finance of the Member States. That of the southern European states led to the establishment of commonplace majority voting, as enshrined in the Single European Act.

Today, predictably, the Commission takes the same line, asserting that 'an enlarged Community will not be able to function effectively without major institutional change. This will in particular affect the Commission, Council and Parliament. The only realistic path for the Community is towards a Federal Europe.'

The European Parliament shares this view. In May 1992, it declared that it would veto the application of any other state unless the 'democratic deficit' was filled and political union strengthened. It is important to remember that 'democratic deficit' does not refer to any notion that the Commission is too powerful, but rather to the idea that too many decisions are taken by the 'unelected' Council of Ministers, and that further powers should be transferred from this body and from national parliaments to the European Parliament at Strasbourg.

The countries whose applications for membership are officially on the table at the time of writing are Austria (which applied as long ago as 1989), Sweden, Finland, Malta, Cyprus and Turkey. The Swiss Government has also submitted its application for membership, but has not yet received the assent in the referendum which it requires for this application to go forward formally. In addition, the Governments of Hungary, Czechoslovakia and Poland have announced their intention to seek membership of the EEC: meeting in Višegrad in February 1991, these three Governments announced that they would apply collectively and as a bloc. Other European countries whose eventual membership is considered possible are Norway and Iceland (two Efta countries currently displaying absolutely no enthusiasm for the EEC), the Baltic states, the former Yugoslav republics, and the other Balkan countries.

Two important factors underpin these applications. The

141

first is the rift between the political leaders and public opinion which has recently characterised the process of European integration. Polls in every Efta country, with the exception of Finland, currently show large and solid majorities against EEC membership, and these majorities have increased since the Danish referendum result in June 1992, especially in Scandinavia. In September 1992, polls in Norway indicated a 49 to 35 per cent majority against membership. In Sweden the majority is 47 to 32 per cent. Yet this feeling is nowhere reflected among the Governments of the Efta countries. Only in Norway is there any significant parliamentary opposition to European integration. Other Efta governments, while they maintain some reservations about specific issues such as farming and neutrality, are apparently content with the *finalité politique*. The Austrian Government is an especially strong advocate of Federalism, while the Governments of the three Višegrad states vie with each other in their unreserved allegiance to the concept of full political union.

The second factor associated, in particular, with the applications from the former Eastern Bloc countries is that of the EEC's trade and tariff policies, which make existence on the doorstep of a protectionist bloc increasingly painful. The EEC pursues the dual policies of denying its markets to goods from these countries while dumping its own subsidised products abroad, policies paid for at considerable cost by its own consumers and taxpayers respectively. The raising of a 'grain curtain' is threatening the economic stability of those countries which have lost the protection they enjoyed from the former Soviet empire.

Consider Hungary as an example. Under current trade arrangements, Hungary is allowed to export 5,000 tonnes of beef per year to the EEC, which is to rise to 6,500 tonnes over the next five years. This compares to some 100,000 tonnes in the mid-1970s sold to a smaller Community. Tight quotas are also imposed on Hungary's steel and textile exports, as they are upon those of the other Višegrad states.

The EEC's attitude is somewhat baffling to the Višegrad trade negotiators: it lectures them on the merits of free trade, while closing its own markets. The Polish chief negotiator has demanded to know why the Community has such problems adjusting to the Višegrad states when it accounts for 56 per cent of their trade and they for 1 per cent of its trade.

Given the existence of these EEC policies, it comes as no surprise that the states which border on the EEC are willing to join on whatever terms they are offered. It is also no surprise that there should be fierce debate within the Community as to when they should be allowed to do so.

The British Government in particular has argued consistently that the new applicants should be admitted with a minimum of delay. France, on the other hand, opposes any enlargement of the Community until the provisions of the Maastricht Treaty have been put into practice and the new powers of the Union, which are to be extended in 1996, have likewise been agreed. Spain, Portugal, Ireland and Greece also oppose an early enlargement, albeit for rather different reasons: they fear that the current transfer of resources to them from the richer countries – above all, from Britain and Germany – might be put at risk, and have made it clear that their support for any growth in the size of the Community is contingent on their receipt of guaranteed levels of Cohesion payments.

To present the debate over time-scale as a 'widening v. deepening' debate is something of an oversimplification. While there are many who fear that the arrival of new members will 'dilute' the political centralism of the Community, there is an equally strong alternative view. Each prior enlargement has, after all, led to a further transfer of power to the EEC's central institutions. The Commission has many allies when it argues that enlarging the Community will provide the impetus necessary for closer political integration.

Specifically, it is argued that a Community with twenty or twenty-five members would need substantial reform in order to operate effectively: agreement among so many would prove too elusive under present forms. The Council of Ministers could not function with so many interests present, and many of its powers would have to be shifted to central EEC institutions. The current system of a rotating Community Presidency would likewise have to be replaced with a central Presidency of Europe.

There are, of course, several pragmatic questions raised by the proposed enlargement of the EEC. The three most often cited are farming, neutrality and the budget.

I discussed the issue of neutrality in the previous chapter: the Commission has demanded that the Efta states agree in advance to abide by a common defence policy which is as yet unspecified, thus provoking some concern among the applicant Governments.

The agricultural question is a more complex one. On the one hand, the Efta countries maintain agricultural subsidies higher even than those of the CAP (albeit considerably more efficient); Finland, which pursues a policy designed to populate its freezing borders with Russia, tops the European league table with levels of support costing its citizens $1,137 per head every year. On the other hand, Hungary, Poland and Czechoslovakia have recently re-formed their agricultural regimes with such rigour that they now have what are effectively free markets in farming. The Commission has commented on this 'problem' in a way which is rather surprising given the stated free-market aims of the EEC:

> There is a contradiction between the trade-liberalisa-
> tion policies undertaken by the Eastern and Central
> European countries and their wish to join an econo-
> mic community. This contradiction arises in areas

144

such as textiles, steel and coal as well as agriculture, but the CAP is its most spectacular manifestation.

Finding a way to include both the Scandinavian and the Višegrad states will be one of the greatest challenges ever to have been faced by the EEC.

The costs of the CAP will soar following the admission of any of these countries, adding to the serious budgetary difficulties which will be caused by the entry of the Višegrad trio. Under the current formula for Cohesion payments, the membership of Poland, Hungary and Czechoslovakia would necessitate a doubling of the present budget. Turkey alone would cost nearly as much.

As is the case with its farming and defence policies, the current budgetary arrangements of the EEC simply could not survive a substantial enlargement of the Community.

Perhaps the most important development in the recent history of the Community has been the creation of the European Economic Area (EEA), to become operative in 1993. Under its terms, the seven Efta states and the twelve states of the EEC have agreed to establish a tariff-free area among themselves, in which the free movement of goods, services, people and capital is assured. The Efta states agreed to make a contribution to the Community budget in return for participation in the market. This figure is far smaller than that which they would make under the terms of 'own resources' were they full members of the EEC. Austria, for example, currently pays 5 billion schillings a year, as compared with what would be a net cost of some 14 billion schillings.

The Efta states remain outside the jurisdiction of the European Court and free from any EEC decisions which do not relate directly to trade.

The creation of the EEA is the result of agreements between governments, and in no way binds its signatories to later decisions which may be made by its own institutions. Many officials, both in the EEC and in Efta, see the creation of the EEA as a form of 'half-way house', which will smooth the way for the eventual entry of the Efta states into the Community. Its creation, however, could mark the beginning of something far more important.

The Efta states now occupy a position within a free-trade area, but outside political union. They have no voice in shaping Community policy , but Community policy is not exercised within their countries. There is no doubt that the majority of Efta citizens, and at least some of their governments, are satisfied with these arrangements. For their part, the EEC states no more wish to deprive themselves of the benefits of wide free trade than do the comparatively wealthy Efta countries. The precedent has thus been set for countries to participate in certain areas of common European interest without accepting all EEC structures and policies in their entirety.

This precedent is enormously important when consideration is given to the likely effects of enlargement upon the Community. It will become increasingly difficult to apply a common agricultural policy to an EEC which includes Cyprus as well as Finland, a common social-welfare policy to an EEC which includes Turkey as well as Germany, or a common border-controls policy to a Community which includes Britain, Malta and Poland.

At present, there is no provision for accommodating this diversity. When a policy is formulated, an executive decision taken, or a judgment made, it is equally applicable in all Member States. The Twelve must go forward together or not at all. The only leeway occasionally permitted to Member States is the ability to choose the means and the pace of implementing a policy: a Commission Regulation is applicable in all Member States equally, while a Directive specifies the end, but leaves the Member States free to adopt the method. This rigidity is regarded as a price worth paying in order to achieve the objective of full integration. The Commission, the Court and the European Parliament have always taken the view that it is more important for 'Europe' to have a common defence, trade, health or dog-registration policy than for this policy to be effective.

This attitude is wholly consistent with a belief in a federal future; without it, the momentum towards integration would simply disappear. Thus, for example, the unanimous response of the EEC's governments and institutions to the Danish referendum in July 1992 was to look for a way to 'accommodate' the Danish Government, to 'bring the Danes back on board'. There was no question of allowing Denmark to continue to accept the terms of EEC member-ship under pre-Maastricht arrangements but to decline to participate in the new extensions of Community authority spelt out in the Treaty on European Union. Had such an option been granted to the Danes, other countries would have demanded similar privileges, and the dream of creating a unitary European state would have become unattainable.

The Member States of the Community have hitherto been prepared to sacrifice effectiveness for uniformity, to replace superior domestic policies with inferior EEC policies for the sake of integration. Yet as the EEC expands, both politically and geographically, the gap between what is the best policy and what is the policy capable of common application will necessarily widen.

The central question regarding the proposed expansion of the Community thus remains that of whether it will provide the impetus for closer integration or for the begin-ning of a Europe 'à la carte'.

In the short term, enlargement will not have a massive effect one way or another. It will bring in several more Governments committed to Federalism and several millions of citizens opposed thereto, thus reflecting existing patterns within the Community. In the longer term, however, the

147

effects will be considerable. There is a general agreement from the most ardent Federalists to their staunchest opponents that the EEC simply cannot continue in its present form. The Federalist solution is to contain the disagreements (which are certain to arise) within a tighter, more centralised structure.

Their proposals have led the Hungarian Trade Minister, Peter Akos Bod, to draw uncomfortable parallels between the Community which his country may eventually be allowed to join and the Comecon which it recently left. Comecon, he points out, was coercive in that a Member State was unable to secede; this is not yet the case within the EEC, but protectionist trade policies make non-membership a very difficult option for largely agricultural countries. Comecon was also centrally planned, replacing free trade with central directives and regulations. It was inflexible, refusing to allow its members to tailor policies to suit their individual needs. Comecon was introverted, denying its members the benefits of open and proper relationships with third countries.

Present EEC legal structures, combined with the changes which are proposed to make enlargement possible, will, Akos Bod fears, lead to the Community making the same mistakes which were made by Comecon.

The alternative to these difficulties is to use the opportunities created by enlargement fundamentally to alter the structures of the EEC. The admission of several neutral countries need not lead to a stifling of their differences within a monolithic defence structure; it could instead lead to a flexible approach to defence, in which individual Member States integrate to the extent that they feel is necessary and beneficial. The combination of Germany's loose asylum laws with 80 million Turks as citizens of the Union need not lead to a rigid common policy on immigration and residence; it might instead lead to a flexible

148

approach to these issues, allowing Member States to adopt policies in accordance with their own national needs. An enlarged Community need not offer similar welfare rights to Swedish and Polish workers; it might instead come to reflect local market considerations within its different member countries.

This flexibility of approach is impossible with the EEC as presently constituted. But public opinion across Europe clearly favours the concept, and will do so with increasing urgency as the difficulty of applying common policies to the entire Continent becomes more visible.

The Commission's stance of responding to enlargement with closer integration is likely eventually to prove unworkable. Its rigorous application of the *acquis communautaire* and the *finalité politique* to new members will in all probability lead to a Europe too full of contradictions to survive as a unitary bloc. These contradictions can, of course, be avoided if they are recognised from the start. The admission of new members to a Europe which allows them to adopt common policies only where they are feasible and productive, and the consequent necessary institutional changes which will allow existing members this option, would bring about the effective development of a 'Europe of varying geometry' in a calm and deliberate fashion.

The challenge is therefore to use the opportunity afforded by expansion to restructure the existing EEC along looser and more liberal lines.

The clamour for this kind of reform is growing across Europe. There are increasing demands that the central institutions of the EEC should be reduced to a minimal role, that Member States should be allowed to integrate only so far as they wish, and that it should be possible for a country to remain within a European free-trade zone, but outside a politically united federation – as Norway, Iceland and the other Efta states have done since the establishment of the EEA.

149

Whether this clamour is loud enough to bring about so fundamental a change in the EEC at the very time when Community institutions wish to move in the opposite direction is a question which needs now to be addressed.

Chapter 9

The Mounting Opposition

I T HAS taken time for people around Europe to grasp the full meaning of what has been done, and continues to be done, in their name by their political leaders. Except in those countries such as Ireland, Greece and Portugal, where the benefits of Federalism are largely measured in terms of the largesse it produces for them, greater comprehension of what is going on has brought growing anxiety about it. This has created a widening gap between the leaders and their electorate. Astonishingly, the list of countries where there is a rising concern includes France, where the European ideal was first generated. Now there are the early signs that in some countries, including Italy, the new disenchantment is turning into active resentment.

By midsummer 1992, according to a poll carried out for the newspaper *The European*, only in three of the twelve countries was there support for the Maastricht Treaty of over 50 per cent. What was especially significant was the size of the 'don't knows', typically some 30 per cent. More recently there has been a steep decline in the support for political union. This is perhaps best illustrated by a brief look at what is happening in Germany, Denmark, the United Kingdom and France, the three largest countries in the Community and the one in which opposition to Maastricht was born.

GERMANY

The position emerging in Germany is interesting and in one sense rather disturbing. Opinion polls for some time have shown a growing mood of disenchantment in Germany with developments within the EEC. Two particular questions are worrying the Germans. The first is the threat which a growing number of them see to the strength and stability of their currency. As early as June 1992 the Wickert Research Institute, from a poll of 4,219 voters, showed that 74 per cent felt that Germany could no longer afford European Union; 81 per cent wanted a referendum on monetary union; 82 per cent of these said that they would be against replacing the Deutschmark with the ECU.

A poll in *Die Welt* at the end of July showed 48 per cent of Germans seeing advantages in EEC membership (compared with 53 per cent in 1991 and 78 per cent in 1990). Two television phone-in polls in June of 1992 produced figures of 81 per cent (ARD station) and 70 per cent (Hesse station) opposing European Union.

The concern for the future of the Deutschmark within the EEC erupted belatedly in the Bundestag in early October 1992; at the insistence of an all-party committee, the Parliament pressed for a second opportunity to ratify stage 3 of the Maastricht Treaty before the Deutschmark became irrevocably part of the Single Currency.

The second problem on the minds of Germans is the perceived invasion of their country by foreigners, especially by those who have arrived as a result of the liberal asylum laws. The growing resentment against foreigners erupted in the summer of 1992 in prolonged periods of violence, much of which was condoned by ordinary residents, on the streets of several large towns. This has not yet turned specifically against the institutions of the EEC. It is, however, illustrative of a growing feeling amongst Germans that their political leaders are out of touch. In this sense it is significant that, unlike in France and Britain, no politician of note has given voice to the growing disquiet in Germany about the move in Europe towards a Federalist state. One wonders to what extent this is due to the fact that through the 'list system' associated with proportional representation, German politicians act very much under the direct control of their party machines. Those in control of the party machines – as in Britain and France – have decided in favour of movement in a Federalist direction.

DENMARK

The first country in which the mood of hostility towards a federal Europe in general and the Maastricht Treaty in particular surfaced in the ballot box was, of course, Denmark. Here there was an 82 per cent turn-out for the referendum which took place on 2 June 1992, when the Treaty on European Union was rejected by 50.7 per cent to 49.3 per cent.

This vote was of the utmost significance. It meant that the Government of Denmark under the premiership of Poul Schlüter was prohibited from ratifying the Maastricht Treaty. Article 20.1 of the Danish Constitution allows powers to be 'delegated to international authorities set up by mutual agreement with other states for the promotion of international rules of law and cooperation'. This, however, is only possible if one of two conditions is fulfilled. Either the Parliament (the Folketing) must pass the appropriate legislation with a five-sixths majority (in the current Parliament requiring 150 members out of a total of 179), or, in the words of Article 20.2 of the Constitution, 'If this majority is not obtained . . . the Bill shall be submitted to the Electorate for approval or rejection'. In the event, the Maastricht ratification bill received only 130 votes in the Danish Parliament. Given the opportunity of a simple 'Yes/No' vote, a majority of the Danish electorate voted against approval of the bill, which was consequently rejected. The Danish veto of the Treaty on European Union is therefore absolute.

The critical significance of this from the point of view of the future of the Maastricht Treaty relates to Article 236 of the Treaty of Rome. The crucial sentences here are: 'The Government of any Member State or the Commission may submit to the Council proposals for the amendment of this Treaty . . . The amendments shall enter into force after being ratified by all Member States in accordance with their respective constitutional requirements.'

The amending Treaty on European Union can become law only if there is unanimous agreement to this effect. The result of the Danish referendum means that the Maastricht Treaty cannot be ratified. It is important to be clear that the people of Denmark did not vote for a modification of the Treaty, as is sometimes suggested. The whole of the text of the Treaty was contained in the bill put before the Folketing. The referendum was a vote on this bill; its rejection meant that Denmark blocked the Maastricht Treaty in its entirety.

The full significance of the Danish vote seems to have escaped the immediate attention of most of the political leaders around Europe. From the start they treated it as something to be 'put right'. On the morning after the result of the referendum had been announced, the British Foreign Secretary went on the BBC's *Today* programme to announce, in effect, 'business as usual' and that the time-

154

table for the passage of the Maastricht ratification legislation by the British Parliament would proceed precisely as planned. By noon on the same day, it is true, the Government had accepted that there had been a slight set-back and that the European Communities Bill would have to be put temporarily on ice, but almost immediately they conceived and put into place a new plan.

In concert with the Governments of the other ten Member States, this was subtly to put pressure on the Danes to change their minds. The strategy was given its first airing two days after the Danish vote at a meeting of the Council in Oslo on 4 June, when it was agreed to proceed with the ratification of the Maastricht Treaty while giving time to the Danes to resolve their problems.

In Britain, ministers were careful to introduce any announcements they made on the matter with assurances that there was no intention to bully Denmark. At the same time it was made clear that British foreign policy was not going to be dictated by the whims of one small country. A way would have to be found by the time of the Edinburgh Summit (later the Birmingham Summit was introduced for the same purpose) of providing a form of words (possibly involving subsidiarity) which would help the Danes to save face.

The prime minister put the Government's position very clearly in a statement to the House of Commons on 3 June, the day after the Danish vote: 'The Government continue to believe that the deal we secured at Maastricht is in the best interests of this country. In the expectation that Denmark will in due course be able to join them, our partners propose to complete the ratification procedures. We share that judgement and intend to continue with the passage of the Bill.'

Later on the same day, in reply to a question, the prime minister added: 'I can certainly confirm that the decision in Denmark is for the Danes and I see no external pressure being put on them; but it is a matter for the Danes and for their Government to decide.'

The problem was that in reality it was not so much the Danes who had to decide – they had already made up their minds – as the remainder of the EEC partners who had to face the consequences of the Danish decision. The French Government's response, as swift and dramatic as it turned out to be highly risky, was to call its own referendum. The British Government, mindful no doubt of the prospect of taking over the Presidency at the end of the month and apparently unaware of the flagging support in the country for Maastricht, pressed on with the approach which had been agreed at Oslo of 'helping' the Danes to change their minds while preserving the Treaty intact.

The approach was based on two specific misconceptions.

The first was the assumption that a 'form of words' which did not amend the text of the Treaty would be sufficient for the Danish Government to be able to claim that it had satisfied the wishes of the people as expressed in the referendum. I have suggested already that neither assurances, nor probably even 'Declarations', are deemed by the Court of Justice to affect the law as defined by the Treaty of Rome, as amended. Anything less than a textual change to the Treaty is therefore no change at all.

Accepting this, some members of the British Government seem to have fallen back on to the second misconception. This was to assume that the Danish people would change their minds of their own volition; that they had been so overcome by the enormity of what they had done that they would hardly be able to wait to get back to the polling stations to put it all right.

The evidence, as expressed in opinion polls held in Denmark since the referendum, is to the contrary; it shows that there has been a hardening of the 'no' vote. It is indeed difficult to understand how the idea gained circulation that the Danes were itching to be allowed to change their minds. As early as the midsummer of 1992, the *Morgensavisen Jyllands Posten* had put the anti-Maastricht vote at over 60 per cent.

The fact is that the opposition of the Danish people to the notion of a Federalist Europe is deep-rooted. The greater the length of time that they have had to consider the full implications of what was proposed at Maastricht, the stronger have been their reservations. Denmark joined the EEC for much the same reasons as the British did: she wished to ensure that she was not excluded from a large 'home' market, particularly for her agricultural products. Like the British, the Danes have watched with growing alarm as the institutions of the EEC have begun to take control of matters far beyond what was thought to be their original remit. Increasing EEC involvement in defence and foreign policy seems to have been of particular concern to the Danes. Above all, they did not take kindly to the notion of becoming citizens of a European Union. They were, and are, especially concerned about what this might mean for the rights to be enjoyed in their country by an ever growing number of Germans who have bought property in the south of Denmark. These anxieties were evidently not assuaged by the inclusion in the Maastricht Treaty of a Protocol on the Acquisition of Property, which preserved the status of Danish legislation with respect to holiday homes. After three wars fought with Berlin in the last 150 years, concern to preserve the sanctity of the border with Germany runs deep in Denmark.

This view has been expressed by, amongst others, the Member of the Folketing, Pia Kjaersgaard, leader of the Progress Party, which was one of the two in the Parliament to oppose the Maastricht Treaty. I recently met Mrs Kjaersgaard in London to discuss our common objective to forge a link between parliamentarians across Europe who wish to see Europe united not by a single government but with a free market. We discussed also the future prospects for the Treaty of Maastricht in both Denmark and Britain.

These had been thought to have been indicated by the British prime minister in a speech at the Queen Elizabeth II Conference Centre in London on 7 September 1992. In this, he had expressed his view of the appropriate approach to the impasse in Denmark thus: '. . . the Danish difficulties must still be overcome. And then across Europe, national parliaments must approve the Treaty.' Some comfort was taken here and in Denmark by the prime minister's use of the phrase 'and then'. This was assumed to mean that before the British Parliament was asked to ratify, there would need to be a clear plan for addressing the Danish veto which was likely to be acceptable to the Danish people. At the end of September, the prime minister held talks with Mr Poul Schlüter, the Danish premier, and apparently concluded from these that the way was clear to reintroduce the European Communities (Amendment) Bill soon after Parliament returned from the summer recess. The Government maintained this position, even after the wide range of options contained in the White Paper published in Copenhagen on 9 October and a contribution made by Mr Schlüter to the special Council of Ministers on 16 October showed that the Danish Government had not even decided in its own mind what position to take.

Meanwhile, the cry from the opposition parties in Denmark, notably the Social Democrats, who comprise the largest party, was for a change to the Treaty which would be legally binding. In other words, mere assurances by heads of government or even 'Declarations' would not do.

The British Parliament is therefore being asked to ratify a Treaty which by the terms of the Treaty of Rome is defunct and which Denmark is likely to wish to see fundamentally changed.

FRANCE

As Europe's politicians reeled from the shock of Denmark's rejection of the Maastricht Treaty, it was François Mitterrand, a fierce promoter of European integration and the Community's longest-serving head of government, who took the initiative in seeking to resuscitate the Treaty. On 3 July 1992 he announced that the French people were also to be given a referendum on the subject of whether Maastricht would be ratified.

M. Mitterrand was well aware that the French electorate was the most *communautaire* in the EEC: the Community had, after all, been created by Frenchmen with French interests in mind and had succeeded admirably in furthering those interests. Germany was locked in, agriculture protected, American influence kept out. France had immense influence in Brussels and a long and happy record of setting the EEC's agenda according to French needs. In these circumstances, M. Mitterrand looked forward to a 'Yes' vote of as much as 70 per cent. Such a result would wipe out the effect of the Danish vote and would, it was hoped, have the side-effect of dividing M. Mitterrand's right-wing opponents.

In the early days of July it seemed that the president's plan could not fail: the leaders of every mainstream party joined the 'Yes' campaign, leaving opposition in the hands of an unholy alliance between the Fascists and Communists. Every national newspaper pressed the case for a 'Yes' vote, with the sole exception of the Communist daily *L'Humanité*. The state-controlled television threw itself vigorously into the fray.

On 1 July a SOFRES poll in *Le Figaro* showed that 69 per cent of those asked predicted a 'Yes' vote. As the summer progressed and copies of the Maastricht Treaty were distributed, understanding of what had been conceded by the politicians began to grow. Across central France, in the *mairies* of small towns, there was a tangible feeling that too much was being given to remote and unelected bureaucrats, that the political class did not speak for France.

It is important to be clear about one thing; contrary to a widely held belief, those who voted 'No' to Maastricht were *not* voting 'No' to Mitterrand. Exit polls on the night of 20 September, largely accurate as to the result, showed that the overwhelming majority of 'No' voters gave 'concern over national sovereignty' as the principal reason for their decision. Only 12 per cent of the 'No' voters – 6 per cent of all voters – admitted that they were voting against the president, and this by no means implies that they would necessarily have otherwise voted 'Yes'. These polls fully bore out my own impressions as an observer of the French campaign: 'No' voters were voting for democracy and for national independence; they were voting against bureaucracy, against technocracy, against what they conceived to be the faulty policies of Brussels. It is a quite mistaken interpretation of the result to assume that the French people were not fully aware of the issue on which they were being consulted.

In the event, the result was extraordinarily close: of 25,678,059 votes cast, 13,081,935 (50.95 per cent) were in favour of ratifying the Treaty on European Union and 12,596,124 (40.05 per cent) were against. For such a result to have occurred in the birth-place of European integration even two years ago would have been unthinkable.

The campaign to oppose Maastricht, which had initially fallen into the hands of the Fascist National Front, led by anti-immigrant Jean-Marie Le Pen, was taken over during the summer by two rebels from each of the mainstream parties of the right – Philippe Séguin from the RPR and Philippe de Villier from the UDF.

Neither Philippe Séguin nor Philippe de Villier is in any

sense a 'flash in the pan'. Each has his own highly developed notion of a free trading market of closely associating nation states. Philippe de Villier is a Député in the Parliament and President of the General Council of the region of Vendée. A former Minister for Culture, he is author of *Pour l'Europe, contre Maastricht*. He has also contributed to several other works on the subject. Here is what he says in *L'Europe Déraisonnable*, published in 1992 by Valmonde:

> C'est l'Europe – fusion de Maestricht, où les nations cèderaient des éléments essentiels de leur souveraineté: monnaie, taux de change, contrôle de l'immigration, définition de la citoyenneté. On nous dit qu'en perdant cette autonomie, nous deviendrons plus forts: en somme, être moins souverain, c'est être plus souverain! Comment peut-on énoncer une telle contradiction?

I first met Philippe de Villier in London on 22 July 1992, when he proposed the concept of a family of European nations, a softer version of de Gaulle's *Europe des patries*.

Philippe Séguin, also a former Minister (Social Affairs), is a member of Jacques Chirac's Rassemblement pour la République Party. Down to earth, where de Villier is more flamboyant, together with Charles Pasqua he was able to muster the anti-establishment vote without rabble-rousing insults. Séguin too has contributed to books on the subject of the Community's future, the latest being *De l'Europe en général et de la France en particulier* (Le Pré aux Clercs, 1992).

He told a key meeting in Dunkirk at the end of August: 'You must find the nerve to ask for a better treaty; one that hands less power to Brussels, controls bureaucracy more stringently and leaves France her autonomy in foreign and monetary policy.'

The two Philippes have proved a powerful combination.

I, and my British Parliamentary colleagues who think as they do, look forward to an increasingly close and warm cooperation with them and with other parliamentarians around Europe who share the vision of a united, free-trading, but not a federal Europe. We have well-laid plans to this effect.

UNITED KINGDOM

The British people have not been allowed to express their views through a referendum, although the trend in opinion as measured by opinion polls has been firmly against a Federalist structure. By 7 September 1992 an ICM poll was showing that only 24 per cent of the British electorate wanted 'to exchange some of our sovereignty for closer ties with Europe', while 76 per cent wanted 'to leave Britain as a trading partner with the rest of Europe'. Sixty-six per cent wanted a referendum on the matter. A poll for the *Independent on Sunday* on 20 September suggested that, were such a referendum to be held, the result would be a 2–1 vote against ratifying the Maastricht Treaty. A MORI poll on 5 October showed 68 per cent against ratification whereas in June and September comparable figures had been 46 per cent and 48 per cent.

In Britain this growing public alarm at the course of events has increasingly found expression in Parliament, especially from the Conservative benches in the House of Commons. This has been particularly true of the Parliament which was returned at the General Election on 9 April 1992. In this House it has been easier for Conservative Members in particular to take a dispassionate view of the matter than was possible for them in the previous Parliament, working as they were under the shadow of a General Election and in the aftermath of a traumatic change in leadership.

The first real indication of the mood of the new House came on Wednesday, 3 June 1992, the day after the Danish 'no' vote and a few hours after the prime minister had told Parliament that he intended nevertheless to press ahead with the bill ratifying the Maastricht Treaty. I remember vividly the response which this evoked among many of my parliamentary colleagues. The sense of relief that the Danes had 'let us all painlessly off the Maastricht hook' was immediately replaced by a despondency at the Government's response. At least, it was felt by many, the Government could have used the occasion to open up new options (to be narrowed again perhaps after the French referendum). They could have said, 'We tried our best. Through no fault of ours the situation has changed. Now we will have to wait and see how matters evolve.' Instead of this, the impression was given by ministers that their previous doubts about the Maastricht Treaty had been swept away by the Danish vote. In their place was a new, albeit frustrated, enthusiasm. Instead of conceiving what had taken place as the best that could be managed in the circumstances, the Treaty had become some sort of model of what needed, come hell or high water, to be put into effect. In response to this new determination by ministers, Government Whips began to huddle together in the Members' Lobby and elsewhere, like American football players in a scrummage, to plan the retrieval process.

I and a few others who only that morning had begun to look forward to a peaceful summer ahead, swiftly concluded that we must make some gesture of our own in order to demonstrate the feelings of many of our fellow conservative Members of Parliament. Within minutes of the prime minister's sitting down at 4.15 p.m., we had constructed the wording of what became Early Day Motion number 174, and which read as follows:

That this House urges Her Majesty's Government to use the decision to postpone the passage of the

> European Communities (Amendment) Bill as an
> opportunity to make a fresh start with the future
> development of the EEC and in particular concentrate
> its efforts on the chosen agenda of the British presi-
> dency which is to extend the borders of the EEC and
> to create a fully competitive Common Market.

The key words, which were later to become something of a
catch-phrase, were 'fresh start'.

Despite their description, 'Early Day Motions' are not
intended for debate at all. Their purpose is to provide
evidence of the strength of a particular point of view
amongst Members of Parliament. The effect of these EDMs
is measured by the number of signatures they attract when
they are printed on the daily Order Paper. Although signatures can be added after the initial printing of the Motion
(and usually are), its impact is judged very much on the
amount of support it receives on first printing. This can be a
major problem for the sponsors of the Motion if there are
not many Members around the House on the day on which
it is decided to 'put the Motion down' or, in other words, to
go public with it.

The challenge with which we were faced on the day of
the 'Fresh Start' Motion was that we knew that a very full
House, which had come to hear the prime minister's Maastricht statement, would deplete rapidly after he was
finished, as the business to follow – a debate on the Earth
Summit – was not very controversial. We had therefore to
move fast. Fortunately it was a warm afternoon and many
colleagues took the opportunity to discuss among themselves the significance of the Maastricht events on the
terrace overlooking the Thames.

With my name heading the list, James Cran, Christopher
Gill and others plunged into the terrace crowd, in addition
to hunting along the corridors and in the committee rooms,

in search of signatures from Conservative Members of Parliament.

It quickly emerged that a good deal of potential support was coming from those Conservative Members who had been elected for the first time. Eventually more than twenty of these added their names. It was then put about by the powers-that-be that, being new, they had not realised the significance of what they were doing. Having personally discussed the matter with many of them, I can vouch for the fact that this was not the case. Almost to a man and woman they are, as it happens, extremely sophisticated individuals, many with a long experience of political activity outside Parliament and several with long-held and well-thought-out anxieties about the course which events were taking in Europe. Each one could have removed his or her name at any time after the first printing and, indeed, two did. Great pressure was put on a number of the signatories to take their names off. The fact that so few complied not only testifies to the courage of those who signed, but also gives the lie to the notion that they were somehow conned into signing or that they did so out of temporary frustration with events immediately following the Danish vote.

It is very understandable that those who wish for a federal Europe should have tried to undermine the credibility of the 'Fresh Start' Motion, since it attracted the names of over eighty Conservative Members of Parliament. (These are listed in Appendix 1.) Many other Members have made it clear that they are supportive but for various reasons do not wish to go public with their views.

In some respects an even more impressive show of feeling was the signing by over seventy Conservative Members of a second 'Fresh Start' Motion following the ERM débâcle. On this occasion some forty colleagues gathered at short notice in Committee Room 9 in the House of Commons on 24 September. We met at 12 noon, prior to the emergency debate on the economy. The group suggested some amendments to a draft motion which I proposed from the chair; the amended motion was then signed en bloc with only two colleagues declining. The wording to which we agreed was as follows: 'That this House welcomes the Government's decision to leave the ERM; and urges a fresh start to economic policy, in particular the abandonment of fixed exchange rates and a commitment to sound finance, stable money and the right climate for steady growth.'

By the end of the afternoon the signatories to EDM 549, listed in Appendix 1, included some very senior members of the parliamentary party, among them several members of the 1922 Executive Committee.

The 'Fresh Start' Motions gained even more significance when over 1,000 representatives to the Conservative Party Conference signed a petition supportive of the first Parliamentary Motion. The precise wording of this Motion was as follows:

I, the undersigned representative to the Conservative Party Conference of 1992, welcome the call in the House of Commons for a 'Fresh Start' in Europe. I support Her Majesty's Government's stated objective of an enlarged, outward-looking, free-trading Community of European nation states and urge the rejection of any moves towards a monolithic, bureaucratic, European superstate.

The views of many Conservative Members of Parliament are much more profound in their objection to certain trends in Europe than it has been possible to encapsulate in any short Motion. What is more, there are many colleagues who did not sign the 'Fresh Start' Motion who have publicly expressed their reservations about developments in Europe.

I present below a short anthology of some of the views of

some present Conservative Members of the House of Commons as they have been expressed in Parliament. These thoughts of my colleagues are significant enough in themselves. Collectively they are evidence of a coherent, deeply felt, formidable body of opinion within the present Conservative Parliamentary Party.

It is a hazardous task at the best of times to categorise the views of parliamentarians, let alone in respect to such a complex subject as the future relationship between Britain and Europe. Nevertheless, in this case I do believe there is some value in tracing differences in the perspectives from which various groups of colleagues seemed to have developed their thinking. Without doubt the strands of thought and philosophy overlap and, especially of late, converge. I present them separately, in preference to an unbroken list, if only for greater ease of reading.

There are first of all those colleagues who for a very long time have consistently held to the view that Britain should not be a part of the Common Market. Roger Moate (Faversham), Sir Richard Body (Holland and Boston) and the Rt Hon. John Biffen (Shropshire North) voted against the Second Reading of the European Communities Bill on 17 February 1972. To their numbers as veterans of the anti-Common Market group must be added Toby Jessel (Twickenham) and Sir Teddy Taylor (Southend East). Each one has held to the view that the Common Market was flawed from its inception, that its membership was not in Britain's interest, that with respect to trade, immigration policy, defence and foreign policy, her true interests were best upheld as an independent nation trading on the high seas. They have been particularly troubled (no one more so than Richard Body) by the distortions and the waste of the Common Agricultural Policy. With the exceptions of Teddy Taylor and John Biffen, of whom more in a moment, each one, because of the strength of his views, has had to eschew a ministerial career, although each would without doubt have made a distinguished holder of office. Each has at least had the consolation, if that is the appropriate word, of seeing some of his worst fears come to pass. Sir Teddy Taylor recently articulated the argument that the anti-Common Marketeers have had to contend with and which has in many respects been found wanting. This is what he said in the Second Reading of the European Communities (Amendment) Bill on 21 May 1992:

> At some stage we must ask ourselves, 'Is this really the EC that we asked people to join?' At the time of the referendum we said to people, 'Do not worry – your powers will be OK; your government is still in charge; democracy is OK; all that we are joining is a free-trade area.' But what have we joined? We have joined a centralised unitary state, and at some stage we shall have to ask the people, 'Do you want to go this way, or do you not?'

Over the years the original anti-Common Marketeers have been joined by several other groups. One of these I will call the 'Constitutionalists'. They comprise those who, having looked hard at the evidence, have become increasingly alarmed at the pace and the direction of the legal and institutional changes which are taking place and which culminated in the Maastricht notion of Union citizenship.

One of the most assiduous, knowledgeable and prominent of the Constitutionalist Conservative Members of Parliament is Bill Cash, Member for Stafford. His book, *Against a Federal Europe*, was published by Duckworth in 1991. It is readable, informative and thought-provoking.

Opposing the Second Reading of the European Communities (Amendment) Bill on 20 May 1992, Bill Cash said, 'My opposition to the Bill and to the Treaty is based on the fact that, under the proposals, we are moving into wholly different territory. The bill is about the future government and democracy of Europe and the United Kingdom. The gravitational pull in the Treaty – which is endorsed by the bill – would take us, indeed drag us, into a federal Europe.' Bill Cash is a lawyer who for many years has specialised in constitutional issues, not least that of the repatriation of the Canadian Constitution.

Undoubtedly one of the most passionate and articulate of the Constitutionalists is Richard Shepherd, Member for Aldridge-Brownhills. In recent months he has made two major speeches in Parliament on the subject. On 21 February 1992, he proposed his own bill to provide for a referendum on the Maastricht Treaty. He spoke brilliantly without notes for half an hour. This is how he ended an equally memorable contribution to the debate on the Maastricht Treaty on 19 December 1991; after restating his belief that the highest form of democracy is 'self-government' through Parliament, he concluded:

> We have watched Eastern Europe grapple for freedom and the liberty that we enjoy, yet I have watched the House of Commons talk solemnly as if this were merely a question of a pile of money at one end of a table or the issuing of financial instruments. It is not – it is about the spirit and life of a nation. I cannot let this go down – sinking – without leastways an exclamation mark and a cry, 'It is wrong.'

Later in the debate, Sir Geoffrey Howe (now Lord Howe), whilst speaking in support of Maastricht went out of his way to congratulate Richard Shepherd on the 'quality of his speech'.

Christopher Gill (Member for Ludlow and a Midlands businessman), as has been mentioned in Chapter 6, has concerned himself for a long time with what were once seen to be obscure constitutional issues of subsidiarity. His more general position is perhaps best summed up by an extract from the speech he made at 3.10 in the morning of 20 May 1992 during the Second Reading of the European Communities (Amendment) Bill. On that occasion he asked:

> . . . are we prepared to put our signature to a treaty which will erode the power and influence of Members of this House to such an extent that they are incapable of delivering the natural and legitimate aspirations of their constituents? Our constituents look to us to obtain redress; if the only satisfaction that we can give them is to say that the matter is out of our hands, it will not be long before they begin to wonder why they voted for us at all.

A very close colleague of Christopher Gill is James Cran (Member for Beverley). Cran and Gill provide much of the organisational back-up for the growing number of parliamentary colleagues who now want to see a 'fresh start' to the future of Europe and the connected economic policy. James Cran rose at 5.17 on the Thursday morning of the Maastricht Bill debate. This is an extract of what he said on that occasion:

> I do not regard myself as a Euro-sceptic. I am very much in favour of Europe. I do not say that we should pull up the anchor and take the United Kingdom somewhere else. We are part of Europe and we must stay part of Europe. I am concerned only about the kind of Europe that we will have.
>
> I wish to see an evolutionary Europe. Institutions are much better if they are allowed to develop slowly. I take exception to the fact that the people who are

deciding matters at intergovernmental conferences want to force the issue of unification far faster than I would wish.

This theme has also been taken up by a new Member who recently made a substantial contribution to the constitutional debate, Ian Duncan Smith, Member for Chingford. He ended a remarkable Maiden Speech on 29 May 1992, which preceded his abstention from the vote on the Maastricht Bill, thus:

> I am not by any means anti-European. After all, Europe is a geographical expression. Therefore, being in the centre of Europe or supporting Europe is neither here nor there. The key is a European Community of nations trading and cooperating through sovereign Parliaments. There is no other time but now. I have talked to many hon. Members who have said, 'Don't worry, this matter will ultimately collapse; things will change and we will not have the problems.'
> If now is not the time to put the line in the sand and say, 'Thus far and no further', when are we to say that? This matter has caused me great concern and problems early in the Parliament, but I hope in the next 24 hours to show where my true attitudes lie.

Next there is a group of colleagues whom I shall describe as the 'Patriots', who through love of country and a proper belief in its democratic institutions do not accept that the time has come to deny our nationality. They include Tony Marlow (Northampton North), John Carlisle (Luton North), Nicholas Winterton (Macclesfield), Ann Winterton (Congleton), Harry Greenway (Ealing North), Bill Walker (Tayside North), Sir Trevor Skeet (Bedfordshire North),

David Porter (Waveney), and Andrew Hunter (Basingstoke).

They each have a tendency to have a very close feel for what the public's 'gut' thinking is on this and, indeed, other matters. They also have an eye for a catchy phrase. This, for instance, is Tony Marlow questioning the prime minister on 3 June 1992 after the Danish referendum result: 'Would my right hon. Friend suggest to Monsieur Napoleon Delors – who today, rather than showing humility, seems to be showing his customary arrogance – that, henceforth, 2 June (the day of the Danish vote) should be a public holiday throughout Europe, to be known as the day of the people, the day of democracy or, even better, the day of the nation state?'

The prime minister answered that he was not sure that he would 'put it that way'.

Here is Nicholas Winterton on the same occasion: 'Will my right hon. Friend the Prime Minister confirm that the "no" vote in Denmark is binding upon the Danish Government?' At that moment this was in some doubt. To have the position confirmed by the prime minister, that it was, was a relief.

This is Sir Trevor Skeet, a very wise and experienced parliamentarian, on 20 May 1992: 'The most extraordinary thing about the United Kingdom is that, traditionally, expenditure and taxation were decided by the House of Commons. This has always been the people's Parliament. In future, these matters will not be decided here because responsibility for many of them may be transferred to Europe.'

I suspect that the colleagues whom I have characterised as Constitutionalists or Patriots may object to the classification as too restrictive of their views. The same will no doubt be true of the group representing another strand of anxiety about what is emerging in Europe: the 'Marketeers'.

The reader may have gathered by now that I place myself

amongst this group. It took me some years after reading economics at Cambridge to form the view that there was no substitute in a free society for the market-place as the most efficient means for encouraging production and for ensuring its distribution. Having for ten years owned and managed one of the most successful econometric consultancy companies in the world (then called Economic Models Limited), I became increasingly disabused of notions for controlling the flow of economic events against their natural movement. I was encouraged in these views through my friendship with several members of the reawakening liberal school of economists. Professor Douglas Hague and Samuel Brittan, whether they knew it or not, had especially strong influences on me. I still regard Samuel Brittan's book *Left or Right, The Bogus Dilemma* (Secker & Warburg, 1968) as one of the most perceptive pieces of contemporary political analysis. It is a source of some sadness to me that I now find myself on the other side of the fence from Samuel Brittan in the debate on managed and fixed currencies. I believe I am merely following along the path which he once trod out.

The parliamentary doyen of the Marketeers is the highly respected former Secretary of State for Trade and Industry and Leader of the House, the Right Honourable John Biffen (Shropshire North). In the nineteen years that I have been in Parliament, I cannot think of anyone, save for Enoch Powell, who has been a more powerful advocate of liberal economics than John Biffen. It is hardly surprising, therefore, that he should view with dismay the return to a managed exchange rate as part of the policy of Europeanisation of the British economy. John Biffen did not sign the 'Fresh Start' Motion, but he has voted consistently against the Maastricht Treaty. This is vintage Biffen on 19 December 1990 in a speech in which he was kind enough to comment favourably on some remarks I had made in Parliament the previous week on the same subject:

> The Government's reluctance to cut interest rates is because of their inhibitions on account of our membership of the Exchange Rate Mechanism . . . I want politicians to be able to form their judgement on what the economy requires and to reach their own decisions on such intimate matters as the rate of interest.

Another parliamentary colleague consistently to make the connection between Britain's economic policies and the European morass into which she is in danger of sinking is Nicholas Budgen, Member for Wolverhampton. Nick Budgen's special skill is in the short, sharp, often witty, question or intervention. During the debate on the Exchange Rate Mechanism on 23 October 1990, he made one of his lengthier contributions. The speech is a gem of lucidity on the subject of managed exchanged rates. This is how he ended it:

> If one was not worried about the sovereignty arguments there might be a case for a single currency in Europe. There is nothing to be said, however, for this half-baked system of the ERM.
>
> Whatever else we do tonight, we should reject the cruel illusion that the ERM is the great magic system that can give the people the stability they desire – in real life we can promise that to no one. If we pretend that that system will bring stability, and if people make commercial judgements in that belief, we will condemn them to bankruptcy, illusion and disappointment.

Another prominent member of the Conservative Party in Parliament who has related the European issue to the economic problems Britain is facing is the former minister and current UK Chairman of Texas Instruments, John

Butcher, Member for Coventry South-West. This is what he told the House on 19 December 1991:

> The Exchange Rate Mechanism is nonsense. Jacques Delors says that floating exchange rates are the grit in the oil. Floating exchange rates are the oil. They take the strain. It is like the differential gear on the back axle of a car. It allows the vehicle to manoeuvre without tearing itself apart on the back axle.

Next I mention the only Member of Parliament at the time of writing to have resigned from a Government position as Parliamentary Private Secretary over the Maastricht issue, Roger Knapman, Member for Stroud. This is what he had to say to Parliament on 20 May 1992:

> I believe in a group of sovereign and nation states cooperating together for their mutual advantage, principally through the means of a single market, regulated as little as possible. That is very different from integration, federalism or union. Silly me – I had thought that that was party policy, but unfortunately there has been some turning of the tide.

All the colleagues I have mentioned so far either abstained or voted against the Second Reading of the Maastricht Bill. A crucial question now is how the mood of the parliamentary Conservative Party has moved since that date.

One way of addressing this is for me to continue to highlight some of the views of colleagues who have not, in the public mind at least, been closely associated with the anti-Federalist cause and several of whom were not, for instance, among the eighty-odd Conservative Members who signed one or both of the 'Fresh Start' Motions. I do not pretend that the following list is comprehensive and I shall give it without much comment, allowing the reader to form his own judgement as to its significance. Before doing so I should say by way of parenthesis that I have totally bypassed the colleagues who are currently members of the Government, several of whom suggested privately that they would resign if the Maastricht bill or anything like it is brought back on to the floor of the House of Commons.

One of the most senior, thoughtful, economically literate and independent-minded members of the Conservative parliamentary party is Sir Peter Tapsell, Member for Lindsey East. Peter Tapsell was unhappy with Margaret Thatcher's premiership and actively supported the cause of Michael Heseltine. Sir Peter's views on European Monetary Union and on the ERM are therefore of special interest, additionally because of his long-standing association with several City institutions. Here is an example from a question he put to the prime minister on 9 July 1992:

> As this country has determined its own money supply for several centuries, why do ministers suddenly find that they can no longer do that without having their hands held by a group of German bank clerks? Has not the time now come for us to leave the Exchange Rate Mechanism, at least until such time as German interest rates are reduced to a level compatible with the needs of the whole of the rest of Europe?

Another eminent Conservative Member with industrial connections who has had long-standing reservations about the course of events in Europe, and who was one of the first to make the link between these and Britain's domestic economic problems, is the Member for the New Forest, Sir Patrick McNair-Wilson. I have already reported his interchange with the prime minister, Margaret Thatcher, on the subject in a different context.

The Chairman of the Select Committee on Foreign Affairs is the former Cabinet Minister the Right Honourable David Howell (Member for Guildford). In the debate on the Second Reading of the European Communities (Amendment) Bill, he gave what was in effect one of the best arguments against a single economic authority that I have heard in Parliament. This is what he said on that occasion:

> When people talk about momentum in the EC, they do not mean what they used to mean when we first joined the Community, which was a momentum towards the market and towards removing barriers and obstacles: they mean momentum towards more central recycling of funds, more vast transfers of resources and more commitment by the central administration to the gigantic merry-go-round of redistribution. That is a dangerous course.
>
> The idea that one first denies to the poorer areas of Europe the opportunity to compete on costs, to move their exchange rates and to operate their fiscal policies in ways which would attract private investment, and then compensates by redistributing funds on a vast scale, is socialism at its silliest.

Another senior Member of the Conservative Party to have expressed his anxiety is the former vice-chairman, Sir Tom Arnold, Member for Hazel Grove. This is what he said on 8 May 1992:

> I believe that our membership of the ERM has had a major influence on the recession in the United Kingdom.
>
> The more we head down the path to a single European voice in the world community, the more likely it

177

is that the Community, as an institution, will take the permanent seat in the United Nations Security Council that we have rightly enjoyed, as have the French, since the United Nations was established.

Sir Rhodes Boyson, Member for Brent North and a former minister, said this, also on 8 May 1992: 'I certainly do not want a common currency or a central bank. Nor do I want to be ruled by the code of Napoleon, against which our ancestors fought in the Napoleonic wars.'

Yet another senior parliamentary colleague, Ivan Lawrence, Member for Burton, a barrister and chairman of the party's Home Affairs Committee, on 21 May 1992 made the most effective critique of the concept of subsidiarity that I have witnessed. The extract from his speech is long, but its contents are important and I feel it merits reproducing in full:

When we add up all the indicators which show that we are moving closer to federal control, and balance them against the number which show that we are moving further away from central control, we are asking ourselves, what is the meaning of subsidiarity? What will that newly defined concept mean in terms of moving either closer to or further away from centralism? That is the item in the shop window which my right hon. Friend the Prime Minister displayed as the main indicator of moving further away.

According to Article 3B, 'the Community shall take action . . . only if and in so far as the objectives of the proposed action cannot be sufficiently achieved by the Member States and can . . . be better achieved by the Community'.

To begin with, that is a very vague concept. If it is thought that it means that any decision should be taken at the lowest possible level, that unfortunately makes me believe that the concept is not all that it is cracked up to be, and for a number of reasons.

First, it should mean – but it does not – that decisions which do not bear on or affect other Member States should remain with the nation state or below. Community action will be allowed wherever such 'objectives of the proposed action', such as a high level of social protection under Article 2, would 'be better achieved by the Community'. Therefore, the concept of centralisation will apply even where something concerns only one Member State if it conforms with the objectives of the Maastricht Treaty.

Second, as the concept is one of developing powers downwards, inevitably it will be the Community which decides the residue decisions with which it does not wish to deal and which should be devolved downwards – the crumbs from the Community table. That may be challenged by the nation states in the European Court, but, as my right hon. Friend the Foreign Secretary conceded this afternoon, that court has usually reflected integrationist tendencies.

Third, subsidiarity applies only to those areas which 'do not fall within the Community's exclusive competence', so it cannot apply to vast areas of law, such as all internal-market measures and probably most of the existing social provisions which apply to the work-place. In other words, it has a most limited scope.

Fourth, although subsidiarity was not defined in the Single European Act, it was certainly understood to be a principle which applied. When the Foreign Affairs Select Committee went around Europe asking how the Act was likely to work, we were told that subsidiarity applied. We kept asking people what it meant, but nobody could tell us. Sunday trading, for

179

example, is something that one would think was a national matter with the subsidiarity rule applying. Yet the Commission has found reason to claim that matter to itself. It says that Sunday trading will have an effect on the importation of goods. Another example is the Social Charter, which we are told is a matter for European Community control because of its potential effects on the competitiveness of business. Therefore, although one might think that hours of work would be a matter for internal national control, it will be dealt with by the Community if it can get the subsidiarity principle interpreted in that way.

Fifth, subsidiarity will not stand in the way of the Community if the institutions want to claim power – as they will. We need only look at the institutions. There are seventeen Commissioners, each with a vested interest in making his or her portfolio as important as possible. They are underpinned by civil servants, who are well-known empire-builders. That is the institution which will be claiming the subsidiarity principle in its favour.

There is the European Parliament, which no one could deny is power-hungry. There is the European Court of thirteen judges who will interpret the rule. They would not be there unless they shared the European ideal and believed themselves to be an integral part of the process of European unity. As my right hon. Friend conceded, they have unashamedly acted as architects of European integration.

Subsidiarity is too vague, and it will be worthless as a protection against expansion to the centre. Subsidiarity may be even worse than worthless, because if people of the intellect of my right hon. Friends the Prime Minister and the Foreign Secretary believe that it will be some protection when in fact it will not, that illusion may lead to a great deal more movement to the centre than they would like to see.

I regret that I have to conclude that the omens for retaining national control of vital areas do not look good.

Richard Alexander (Member for Newark) has a reputation for thoughtfulness. He is certainly not someone who is thought to 'go over the top'. Here are some words of his on 20 May 1992:

> One of my greatest frustrations is having to tell my electors, in correspondence and personally, that there is nothing I can do about a proposal because a decision has already been taken somewhere else – albeit by ministers, one of whom is a Member of the House – that there is nothing that anyone can do because the decision has been taken outside these shores, so there is no point in writing to me.
>
> It would be reprehensible to extend the concept of ministerial decision to Commission decision. It would emasculate our position as Members of Parliament and it would deprive the decision-makers of that essential element in any democracy – accountability to those who put us here.

Similarly, Andrew Hargreaves, Member for Birmingham Hall Green, is rightly thought to be very 'balanced' in his views. This is what he said in the Second Reading of the Maastricht bill:

> To put my view on the record, I have read the Treaty. I do not yet understand it, but although I was once a keen and proud European, there are things in it that would now make me one of the most sceptical. I therefore give due notice to the Government Whips

181

who are on duty that when we examine the bill in Committee and consider some of the things that are set out in this illustrious treaty, I may not be able to support the Government.

Here is Michael Lord, Suffolk Central, in the same debate: '. . . I am being asked to believe, and to sell to my constituents, the idea that binding us even closer together will one day result in all these inequalities being removed. I do not believe it, they do not believe it and the House should not believe it.'

Here also is a new Member, Nick Hawkins (Member for Blackpool South and a leading member of the Bow Group): 'From my involvement in European matters, I believe that I should say that I have great misgivings about the decision I will ultimately make tonight to support the Government and to support the Maastricht Treaty. I regard myself as sceptical about the ambition of various Commission officials to move towards a more federal state and to subsume Britain's independence.'

Nick Hawkins is representative, as we know from the signatures to the 'Fresh Start' Motion, of many of the new Members.

There are many others whose anxieties about the course of events in Europe are well known. They include Sir Nicholas Fairbairn (Perth and Kinross), Sir Nicholas Bonsor (Upminster), John Townend (Bridlington, chairman of the party's Finance Committee), Michael Carttiss (Great Yarmouth), Rupert Allason (Torbay) and Teresa Gorman (Billericay). To their number must be added the Right Honourable Kenneth Baker (Mole Valley), former chairman of the Conservative Party, who has held many high offices of state, including that of Home Secretary. On 4 September 1992 Ken Baker wrote in the *Daily Express* in advance of the French referendum, 'Courage, mes braves, votez "non".'

I shall not attempt to draw too explicit a conclusion as to what all this adds up to: that will have to be left to historians. From the perspective that I write, I can only take matters as I find them. In order to find them, I have merely thumbed through the pages of recent editions of Hansard. All I will permit myself to say is that there clearly exists a coherent body of thought within the present Conservative Parliamentary Party (supported, it would seem from the number of signatures added to the 'Fresh Start' petition circulated at the 1992 Conservative Party Conference, by a large number of members in the country), which is increasingly concerned by the direction of events in Europe and which makes the connection between this and Britain's recent economic woes.

It would be wrong to leave the subject of the mood on European matters within the British Parliament without reference to the Labour Party.

For thirty years the Labour Party has conducted a debate over the EEC somewhat different from that which has recently emerged within Conservative circles. Labour anti-Marketeers were motivated by two distinct ideologies. The first was the belief in sovereignty and democratic self-government as represented by such figures as the Right Honourable Peter Shore (Bethnal Green and Stepney). The second was a reaction to the concept of the EEC as a 'rich man's club', discriminating against its own poor through the CAP and through its VAT rates, just as it discriminated against poorer countries elsewhere in the world. This view, represented by, for instance, Dennis Skinner (Bolsover), holds that the capitalist mechanisms of the EEC prevent Britain from adopting a socialist programme aimed at creating full employment. These two positions are not, of course, incompatible. They are combined in, for instance, the thinking of Tony Benn (Chesterfield), who has consistently opposed the EEC since 1972.

Set against these anti-Marketeers have been the Labour

Euro-enthusiasts. For many on the Left, the European Economic Community has appealed to a certain brand of internationalism which found expression in hostility to the nation state. Moreover, throughout the 1980s, when opposition to European Federalism became closely associated with Margaret Thatcher, enthusiasm for Europe became a way of protesting against Conservative economic liberalisation.

Yet it was a change in the shape of the EEC itself which was most directly responsible for the most recent shift in Labour's attitude. In an article in the *Sunday Times* on 9 August 1992, Roy Hattersley wrote: 'During the past ten years, Labour has been converted to Europe because Europe has been converted to socialism.' There was, in fact, a social element present in the Treaty of Rome itself, but Mr Hattersley had a point when he suggested that the last ten years saw capitalism and the pursuit of free trade relegated within the EEC to a secondary position. Labour has now moved to a position of adopting EEC laws and institutions as weapons against Conservative economic policy. One has to concede that successive Conservative Governments have accepted rulings from Brussels on, for example, social policy, the regulation of working practices and the straightforward geographical reallocation of wealth which it would be hard to imagine ever having been proposed as part of a domestic Conservative programme.

Set against Labour's attraction to the recent elevation of socialism in the EEC is their dislike of the threat to employment posed by the Exchange Rate Mechanism. Opposition to a fixed European exchange rate has a long history within the Labour movement. The Labour Government's pamphlet *Britain's New Deal in Europe,* issued before the 1975 referendum, stated unequivocally that 'there was a threat to employment in Britain from the movement in the Common Market towards an Economic and Monetary Union. This could have forced us to accept fixed exchange rates for the pound, restricting industrial growth and so putting jobs at risk. This threat has now been removed.' In 1986 Neil Kinnock described the ERM as a 'strait-jacket' which 'would leave us with either a very unstable currency or very unstable interest rates'. Today, Labour opposition to the ERM is led by Bryan Gould, whose Euro-sceptic opinions re-emerged during the contest for the Labour leadership in early 1992. In August Mr Gould called on Labour to back the devaluation of the pound within the ERM and to oppose the ratification of the Maastricht Treaty.

After repeated attempts to bring the shadow Cabinet around to his opposition to the 'permanent deflation and lack of democracy' implied in the Maastricht Treaty, Mr Gould resigned from the shadow Cabinet on 27 September 1992, saying that his wish to speak out on the Maastricht Treaty was incompatible with the burden of collective responsibility, and claiming that over one hundred Labour MPs supported his position.

How strong this support will prove to be in the last analysis remains to be seen, but Labour's treatment of Mr Gould and its refusal to back calls for a referendum on the Treaty suggest that any hopes of altering the movement towards European Federalism remain with the Conservative Party.

Chapter 10

Time for a Fresh Start

I HAVE argued that the exposure of the Federalist position at Maastricht was an event of the utmost historical significance. So far I have left open the question of whether Maastricht is likely to prove to have been the high-water mark of European Federalism or merely a bench-mark against which to test future movement towards a Federalist state.

What happens now depends upon the resolution of two issues. There is first of all the question as to whether the EEC through a Single Currency will become an economic union, as directly proposed by Maastricht, or whether, to the contrary, its members will direct their energies into becoming a closely knit association of free-trading independent nation states.

Second, there is the issue of what is to happen to Lord Denning's tidal wave of European law, crashing the national barriers and submerging the legal and constitutional independence of the nation state. Is it already too great a force to be withstood?

There are those who do indeed believe (as we have seen,

with some justification in terms of legal precedent) that matters have already gone too far in the direction of a United States of Europe for the process to be stopped from reaching its federal point of destination.

I am not one of them. I have consistently maintained the position throughout this book that sovereignty has not yet changed hands. I am persuaded by the majority of legal opinion, which suggests that Britain, her people and her political leaders retain ultimate control over their own destiny. This means that the essential choices are left open; above all, it means that what has already been done is not yet irrevocable.

Let me put this proposition to the test and see what it means first for the future economic character of the EEC and for Britain's place within it. Specifically, what is to be done about the Single Currency and the related issue of the ERM?

In Chapter 5 I suggested two main arguments against the creation of a Single Currency in Europe. The first was that the abrogation of responsibility by a nation for its coinage would be for it to surrender the essence of its own state-hood. A Single European Currency would predetermine the creation of a federal political union and the abolition of the nation state for which, I suggested in Chapter 6, the countries of Europe were not ready. Second, because of the asymmetrical nature of the economies of Europe, a Single Currency would slow down economic growth in Europe. Those countries that could not 'keep up' with Germany or which were on a different economic cycle from her would suffer badly in terms of their standards of living.

Several independent and authoritative bodies and people have recently confirmed the potentially damaging economic impact of a Single Currency on the Members of the EEC. The International Monetary Fund has indicated that it would mean slower growth. In its 1992 *Annual Report*, the Bank for International Settlements, normally very reluctant to enter into any form of political controversy, said this: 'Whether a Monetary Union, which is essentially viewed as a stepping-stone to political union, should be presented as a necessary extension of the programme for completing the internal market in the Community seems questionable.'

Martin Feldstein, Professor of Economics at Harvard University, head of America's Bureau of Economic Research and former chairman of the Council of Economic Advisers to the President of the United States, summed up his views on the matter thus: 'My judgment is that a Single Currency for Europe would be a liability.' Why? Because Feldstein can see only one possible economic benefit, that of removing the cost for businesses and tourists of having to change their money. Against this must be weighed the economic instability which will occur as countries lose the ability to manage their economies according to their own individual needs.

The first conclusion I reach, therefore, is that a Single European Currency is not in Britain's interest nor, as it happens, of that of the other countries of Europe. Britain should therefore not hesitate to use whatever powers and diplomatic skills she possesses to ensure that it does not come about.

The next question is what this decision would mean for Britain's aspiration to regain membership of the European Exchange Rate Mechanism. Many commentators have tried to draw a distinction of economic principle between the ERM and a Single Currency. Clearly there is a difference – in political terms a fundamental one – between exchange rates which are fixed for ever, the essence of a Single Currency, and those which are managed but capable of some adjustment, the ERM. In each case, however, the objective is to replace a process by which the value of one currency against that of another is essentially a reflection of the relative strengths of the economies which lie behind them, with a system for artificially 'holding' the price of the currency. In this sense the ERM and the Single Currency are different points on a continuum leading to the loss of all control by a government over the value of its currency.

In the case of the ERM, where currencies are capable of moving against each other, they are inhibited from doing so outside the chosen bands, either as a result of the country whose currency is under pressure putting up its interest rates (in the hope of attracting buyers to its currency) or through the buying of the weak currency by central bankers. In the case of the Single Currency, the weak country is forced into similar deflationary policies in order to try to depress its unit costs so as to enable it to compete against the strong countries. In the case of both the ERM and the Single Currency, the weak country is at the mercy of the strong one and is forced to run policies which may well be diametrically against its own interests.

The ERM is sometimes justified as a means for beating the currency speculator. The reverse is the case. The ERM serves to focus the minds and to whet the appetites of the speculators. A currency which gradually adjusts up or down over a period of time, depending on the intrinsic strength of the economy which supports it, is much less likely to attract the eye of the speculator than one which is about to burst the artificial dam which has been built around it. Speculators are positively magnetised to situations which they believe to be contrary to the product of natural forces and as a result will not last. They are doubly attracted when it is clear to them that any movement will be all one way, and where all they have to do is to bide their time and wait for the inevitable profits.

All this was particularly noticeable in the summer of 1992 when billions of pounds (some say as much as £20 billion) of foreign reserves (£7.2 billion of which had been especially borrowed for the purpose) were spent by the Bank of England in a vain attempt to prop up the exchange value of sterling.

There is a sense in which membership of the ERM means belonging to the worst of two worlds where there is neither the absolute assurance against speculation provided by a Single Currency, nor the prospect of stable and gradual (and thus for the speculator uninteresting) adjustment of a freely floating exchange rate.

The ERM can only be justified as a stepping-stone towards a Single Currency. Once a decision has been made not to aim for 'irrevocably fixed exchange rates', the ERM loses all point and credibility. A decision to veto a Single Currency must therefore be accompanied by one permanently to leave the ERM. Britain's membership of it has already done the untold harm to the British economy that I described in Chapter 5; the quicker the Government decides to abandon the objective of re-entering the ERM and to take back permanent control of the economy the better.

The idea that the British Government is incapable of running sound financial policies without having them forced upon it through the mechanism of the ERM is an outrageous one. It is an argument against democracy itself. What is more, in Britain in the 1980s it was the other way round. It was only when the Government decided to shadow the Deutschmark that it dropped its commitment to sound money. Furthermore, the constraints of the ERM themselves proved inflationary as increased borrowing by the Bank of England – in order to fund the intervention buying of sterling – had itself to be supported by the issuing of Treasury bills which increase banks' reserves and therefore their capacity for further borrowing.

For most of this century Britain has been obsessed with the idea of holding the price of its currency above its natural value. The Gold Standard, Bretton Woods, the Sterling Area, the unofficial Deutschmark peg, and the ERM have all provided both the means and the excuse for doing so. The effect has been that for most of this century Britain has had to hold interest rates higher than has been necessary or desirable. The high cost of capital in Britain has been a major contributory cause over many years to relatively poor investment levels and low productivity in comparison to many of her competitors. This in turn has resulted in the downward trend in the value of her currency. It is surely time that this process was reversed: cheap capital should be allowed to lead to higher productivity, which in its turn should push a liberated sterling upwards.

At the time of writing, the prime rate is 8 per cent and the rate of inflation is under 4 per cent. With unemployment rising steeply, some say towards four million, and money supply flat, interest rates should be reduced by some 2 per cent.

The time will rapidly approach, however, no doubt just as interest rates are finally reduced to match a reduction in German interest rates (if the pound remains attached formally or informally to the Deutschmark) when the correct policy will be to raise interest rates.

One of the extraordinary features of British economic management over the past fifty years has been the inability of those in charge to comprehend the workings of 'lags': the time it takes for the effect of a change in policy to work through the economy. Because so few of the policy-makers have had direct experience of business, they seem to find it impossible to believe that when, for instance, interest rates fall, the positive effect on business confidence and hence on investment decisions may take up to three years to work through.

It is not good enough, therefore, to operate monetary policy merely by reference to what is going on outside the window on a particular day. There has to be anticipation. Without it, 'Stop–Go', as it came to be known in the 1960s, will be with us for ever. To be able to take action ahead of time requires above all the freedom to do so, unfettered by exchange-rate restrictions.

Quitting the ERM permanently will have one important

psychological effect: it will remind Britain's traders that their destiny is to sell where their market is strongest. There is no moral imperative to sell or to buy in Europe. If the barriers to trade in the EEC are removed and it makes sound economic sense to do so, well and good. But it would be well for British business to remind itself occasionally of the message contained in Figure 1 (page 60): the fastest-growing markets are not in Europe. What is more, the countries of Europe who are not members of the EEC have increased their trade at least as fast as have those of the Community, and there is no EEC country other than Luxembourg which has a per capita income higher than any (except Austria) of the Efta countries. After Luxembourg, Denmark currently has the highest standard of living measured by gross domestic product per head. This stands currently at about $22,000 (ahead of France at around $20,000) and is exceeded by Norway, Sweden, Finland and Switzerland. Austria, at $19,240, has a higher per capita income than Germany ($18,970) or the United Kingdom ($16,070). It would seem, therefore, that there is some sort of life to be eked out in the dark world on the periphery of the EEC even before the foundation, hopefully in 1993, of the European Economic Area by which 380 million people of Efta and the EEC are to join forces to provide one 'home market'.

I do not conclude from this that Britain should leave the EEC. I merely note that other European countries have found an alternative way of living which, as it happens, for whatever reason, has resulted in their enjoying higher standards of living than on the whole do EEC members. What is more, they have all now established the basis for free-trading links with the EEC. In Britain's case it also remains true that she has to make up in sales to the world outside the EEC that which she loses by running a heavy deficit with the Community. When she fails to do this, she runs the heavy overall current-account deficit which it has been her misfortune to do of late.

The Danish blocking of Maastricht has at least made it possible for Britain to argue for 'no Single Currency' and to suspend her membership of the ERM, an option formally closed by the Treaty. The question is whether in view of the power and the momentum of the Commission and the Court of Justice, it is still possible for similar barriers to be placed in the way of the incoming flood of EEC law. For this to be conceivable a specific decision must be taken by the British Government that Britain will not be party to political union in Europe. Such a decision would need to be clearly defined in terms of a line dividing what was acceptable from what was not. For those matters which fall above the line, there can be debate and compromise; for those that do not there cannot. 'Giving in' to prevent 'giving more', which has been in reality the basis of much of British diplomacy in Europe, will need to be replaced by a position which says, 'Above the line anything goes; below it we walk away.'

The brand of political union which is being proposed for Europe is particularly hard for Britain to accept. The fact is that there is a fundamental difference in the philosophy which lies behind the British Constitution and those of her Continental partners.

The distinction is between the Continental concept of the 'universal rights of man', innate and natural rights which it is the duty of the state, bound by the Constitution, to safeguard on behalf of the citizen, and the British concept of the 'rights and liberties of the freeborn Englishman', hard won and historically based rights which it is the duty of the citizen himself to defend from Government encroachment. It is the difference, in Rousseau's terms, between the 'general will' and the will of all; it is the difference between Rousseau's social contract and Locke's society formed to protect individual liberties, between Hegel's notion of the individual as subordinate to the state and the 'individualist' philosophies of the British empiricists, moralists and utilitarians: Hume, Adam Smith, John Stuart Mill and Jeremy Bentham, ranged against Kant, Hegel, Marx and Engels. It is the distinction which exists between common law and Roman law.

Who is to say which is the 'better' tradition? One has led to the written constitution, but it has also led to revolution and at times tyranny. Britain alone in Europe, it has to be said, has a record of parliamentary democracy untouched by dictatorship or revolution. It is hard to see what Britain would have to gain by exchanging her political system for one based on Continental theory and philosophy. Indeed, there is an incompatibility between the British system of democracy and what is emerging in Europe. In particular, the doctrine of parliamentary sovereignty which lies at the root of British democracy cannot be squared with European political union as it is currently proposed. Parliamentary sovereignty allows for there to be no limit on the power of the people's elected representatives in Westminster.

A refusal by Britain to accept political union in Europe will require the renegotiation of certain crucial parts of the Treaty of Rome.

It is necessary to start with the Commission. While the powers of the Commission to initiate policy may be conceived of as those normally possessed *de facto* by an unelected civil service, the powers of interpretation and of law-making are in a true democracy the preserve of the judiciary and elected legislature. I will not rehearse again my reasons for believing that the European Parliament is incapable of filling this democratic void and that for the foreseeable future the elected legislature should remain in national hands. At this point I merely suggest that there should be an amendment to the Treaty of Rome, stripping the Commission of its powers to issue of its own initiative interpretative, law-making directives and making it, as with all democratically controlled civil services, the servant

194

of the elected national governments. Ultimate power must specifically and clearly be returned to the Council of Ministers who directly represent the interests of the various sovereign governments. The Commission would exist essentially to carry out the bidding of the Council.

As to the judiciary, the Court of Justice, this is a more complicated matter. At one level it is a question of ensuring that its judgments are reflective of a genuine balance between the collective interests of the EEC and those of the nation state. The argument has been made by Martin Howe and others that this will obtain only if an appeal court is superimposed above the Court of Justice. The point, which I find persuasive, is that an appeal court which will be less full-time than the Court of Justice will be less imbued with the centralist perspective, and thus in a better position to maintain an objectivity as between the interests of the EEC and those of the nation state.

This is of course to beg the question of where the dividing line between the interest of the nation state and that of the EEC is to be drawn. I am quite clear in my own mind on this. The 'bottom' line is the one that separates those measures which lead to the loss of nationhood from those which are concerned with effecting closer association and cooperation – and freer and fairer trade – between genuinely independent states. Britain is particularly vulnerable in this matter because she does not have a written constitution.

What needs to be done is not as hard to conceive of as is sometimes suggested.

First of all, the principle of the supremacy of national parliaments needs to be firmly established. In Britain's case this requires a specific Act of Parliament. It also requires amendment to the Treaty of Rome. There must be a clear statement in its ultimate that no EEC body, Council, Commission or Court, shall be able to override legislation passed by national parliaments. Clearly this would mean that nothing should be done with respect to the EEC which was legally irrevocable. This itself would rule out the move to a Single Currency. Parliament would also retain the ultimate right to cancel or vary a part or the whole of Community law as it applied to the United Kingdom.

Second, I agree with the suggestion made by Martin Howe that there should be an express list laid down by national parliaments of protected matters which no Community law should be allowed to affect. Such a list would comprise the constitution and procedure of Parliament, including the mechanism for electing it and its sovereign right to raise taxes, the relationship between Parliament, the executive and the courts, and matters to do with defence and foreign policy. It would include, in my view, immigration policy and other matters of internal, purely national interest such as planning and employment procedures and practices.

To sum up, there is a need for a bill to guarantee the supremacy of Parliament. There is also a need for the associated amendments to the Treaty of Rome not only to guarantee the sovereignty of the nation state but also to reform the institutions of the EEC – especially the Commission and the Court of Justice – in the way that I have proposed.

Any amending Treaty of the kind I have described will without doubt demand great skill on the part of the British negotiators; it should be remembered, however, that both the EEC's trade realities and European public opinion are on their side. The acceptance of a bottom line, something that seems to have been singularly missing in the British negotiating stance, will provide its own discipline.

The problem is that time is not on the side of those who wish to maintain the integrity of the nation state. Left to itself, the momentum of the Community legal system will do the Federalists' task for them, with or without Maastricht. As we have already seen, at least one Act of

Parliament has been overridden by Community law.

We are close to the bottom line today. Some say we have already crossed it. In this case, the nation state will have ceased to exist. The concern then must be that when people start to suffer the rule of the power which has replaced the national government, their resentment against not having been warned of the full consequences of what was happening to them will boil over into a form of open rebellion. There are signs that this may indeed be what is happening in Germany.

It is one thing for the British elector to be told by Brussels where British fishermen can fish, or what sort of sausage he can eat. That is on the one hand remote and on the other ridiculous. It is quite another matter to be told what taxes to pay and how much unemployment is to be suffered and then as an afterthought to be informed that there is to be no democratic redress. To point this out is not to be 'negative' or 'anti-European' or 'Euro-sceptical'. On the contrary, it is to yearn for closer unity to be built on firm foundations and to reflect the real desires of a complex patchwork of different nations and of peoples who live in that part of the world geographically known as Europe.

How then do matters rest and where do we go from here?

The present position is one in which the Treaty of Maastricht cannot be ratified because of the Danish veto. The Danish prime minister, Mr Poul Schlüter, has made it clear that he will not initiate a further referendum on the basis of the existing text. The Treaty will therefore have to be amended. In order to be 'Court of Justice proof', this amendment will have to take the form of a change in the primary text of the Treaty or of the inclusion of an additional protocol. In either event, the Treaty will be different from the one currently before the British House of Commons.

Since the Danish Government does not intend to hold another referendum before the summer of 1993, there is at the moment of writing some time left for cool deliberation by parliamentarians as well as by the public they serve.

Those parliamentarians across Europe who wish to see Europe united as an association of freely trading and co-operating independent states must take advantage of this breathing-space to gather together to form a common front. This we shall certainly do, in the firm belief that it is the true way forward – based on a realistic appraisal of the continued role of the nation state – towards peace, stability and prosperity in Europe. The hiatus over the Maastricht Treaty caused by the Danish veto provides the leaders of Europe with perhaps their last chance to reject once and for all the notion of political integration.

I hope and believe that the United Kingdom will take the lead in reforming the Community. Let us dismiss the notion that a free, democratic and outward-looking Community is somehow a perverse Anglo-Saxon concept which divides Britain from the rest of Europe.

All the evidence suggests that, when consulted, the people of Europe have a vision far closer to de Gaulle's loose 'Europe à l'anglaise' than to M. Delors' unitary state. The United Kingdom's negotiators must alter the attitude with which they have approached the question of integration to date: considering as 'victories' what are at best delays in the advance of Federalism, and being willing, at the last, to go along with any formula of political union as an alternative to being 'relegated' to an 'outer tier' of the EEC.

Since joining the Community, Britain has made a consistently disproportionate contribution to the budget; her consumers have largely subsidised the Common Agricultural Policy; her fishermen have lost their stocks to the Common Fisheries Policy; her trading partnerships with the rest of the world have suffered; and she has subsidised the exports of the other member states with a cumulative trade deficit of £86 billion. On balance, I believe that Britain's membership of the EEC has been of some benefit in terms of the home market which she has gained and will continue to gain as and when her partners honour their commitments to complete the Single Market; however, as should be clear from the figures quoted in Chapter 5, the assertion that EEC membership has been good for Britain is open to question. What is beyond question is that British membership has been good for the EEC; not only do British taxpayers and consumers bear the cost of the CAP, the CFP, the Common External Tariff and the Cohesion budget, but Britain constitutes an artificial captive market for the exporters of the Eleven. Britain's negotiating position is thus extremely powerful. It is difficult to see why she has hitherto accepted the development of a unitary European state, which is as distasteful to Continental as to British voters, for fear of being 'left out'.

What, indeed, is Britain being 'left out' of? Behind the grandiloquent phrases about being 'relegated to the outer darkness' or 'consigned to the outer tier' stands a surprisingly simple political question: should the United Kingdom join France, Germany and Benelux in adopting a Single Currency without delay? Even assuming that the French public can be persuaded to accept what will in effect be the Deutschmark as their currency, and are willing to allow their economic policy to be decided by German domestic needs, will membership of this 'inner core' in fact be beneficial for Britain?

As I suggested in the previous chapter, the creation of the European Economic Area and the looming enlargement of the Community make possible the development of an EEC consisting of some twenty to twenty-five freely cooperating nations. If five or six of these states choose to federate within a tight structure governed by a central bank, is it imperative for the United Kingdom to join their Federation? The truth is, judging from the current record of the EEC, that countries which wish to expand its powers against those of their own parliaments, are likely in so doing to extend bureaucracy, regulation and uncompetitiveness.

There exists, then, a place for Britain within a loose European commonwealth, with a free currency and a floating exchange rate, and with a liberal approach to the market rendering her (in the words of Jacques Delors) 'a paradise for investment'. Britain would, in these circumstances, also enjoy full democracy and self-government. This hardly constitutes relegation to a second tier.

I have sought to demonstrate in this book that an attempt to alter the shape of Europe by compromising with the 'Maastricht philosophy' must necessarily end, by faster means or by slower, with the political centralisation of the Community. Given her negotiating strength, Britain is capable of reversing the currently continuous and self-powered process of integration. All that is needed is a positive approach and an end to the specious fear of isolation. If an 'inner core' of countries wish to 'pool' their sovereignty, that is a matter for them: the British public will not feel that losing national control of their employment, health, environmental or immigration policies is counterbalanced by an ability to regulate those policies in Belgium or Germany – the reality of inclusion in a tight 'first division' in Europe.

Nor will public opinion elsewhere in Europe long tolerate such an arrangement. In leading the transformation of the EEC, Britain would place herself in a true sense at the heart of Europe.

What is required is a fresh start in Europe, a new vision of a confident, outward-looking, interlocking commonwealth of democracies, the very opposite of a continent of people sullenly subservient to unelected and anonymous officials operating from some distant and foreign city – the future lot of the citizens of Europe unless the process is consciously and rapidly redirected.

Appendix 1

The 'Fresh Start' Motions

THE FOLLOWING is a list of the Conservative Members of Parliament who signed the two 'Fresh Start' Early Day Motions. The six 'sponsors' are given first. Those who signed but subsequently deleted their names are added with the date of their withdrawal given in brackets.

Early Day Motion Number 174
Future Development of the EEC   First published 3 June 1992

That this House urges Her Majesty's Government to use the decision to postpone the passage of the European Communities (Amendment) Bill as an opportunity to make a fresh start with the future development of the EEC and in particular to concentrate its efforts on the chosen agenda of the British presidency which is to extend the borders of the EEC and to create a fully competitive common market.

Mr Michael Spicer

Mr Barry Legg

Mr Michael Fabricant

Mr James Cran

Mr John Butcher

Mr Nirj Joseph Deva

Mr Peter Ainsworth
Mr Richard Alexander
Mr Rupert Allason
Sir Thomas Arnold
Mr Vivian Bendall
Dr John G. Blackburn
Sir Richard Body
Sir Nicholas Bonsor
Mr Hartley Booth
  (Withdrawn 3.6.92)
Sir Rhodes Boyson
Mrs Angela Browning
Mr Nicholas Budgen
Mr John Carlisle
Mr William Cash
Mr Michael Clark
Mr Geoffrey Clifton-
  Brown
Mr David Congdon
Mr Geoffrey Dickens
Mr Den Dover
Mr Alan Duncan
Mr Iain Duncan-Smith
Mr Bob Dunn
Mr David Evans
  (Withdrawn 11.6.92)
Mr Nigel Evans
Mr David Faber
Mr Liam Fox
Mr Peter Fry
Mr Phil Gallie
Sir George Gardiner
Mr Christopher Gill
Mrs Cheryl Gillan
Mrs Teresa Gorman
Mr Harry Greenway

Mr John Greenway
Mr Peter Griffiths
Mr Nick Hawkins
Mr Warren Hawksley
Mr Charles Hendry
Mr James Hill
  (Withdrawn 29.6.92)
Mr John Horam
Mr Andrew Hunter
Mr Bernard Jenkin
Mr Toby Jessel
Mr Robert B. Jones
Mr Roger Knapman
Mr Ivan Lawrence
Mr David Lidington
Mr Michael Lord
Lady Olga Maitland
  (Withdrawn 4.6.92)
Mr Paul Marland
Mr Tony Marlow
Sir Patrick McNair-
  Wilson
Mr Roger Moate
Mr James Pawsey
Mr Barry Porter
Mr David Porter
Mr Andrew Robathan
Mr Raymond S.
  Robertson
Mrs Marion Roe
Mr William Ross
Mr David Shaw
Mr Richard Shepherd
Mr Michael Shersby
  (Withdrawn 15.7.92)
Sir Trevor Skeet

Mr Anthony Steen
Mr John Sykes
Sir Teddy Taylor
Mr Roy Thomason
Mr John Townend
Sir Gerard Vaughan
Mr Bill Walker
Mr Nigel Waterson

Mr John Watts
Mr John Whittingdale
Mr John Wilkinson
Mr David Willetts
Mr David Wilshire
Mrs Ann Winterton
Mr Nicholas
  Winterton

Early Day Motion Number 549
Fixed Exchange Rates   First published 24 September 1992

That this House welcomes the Government's decision to leave the ERM; and urges a fresh start to economic policy, in particular the abandonment of fixed exchange rates and a commitment to sound finance, stable money and the right climate for steady growth.

Mr Michael Spicer
Mr John Townend
Mr Bob Dunn
Mr Bernard Jenkin
Sir George Gardiner
Sir Rhodes Boyson

Mr Rupert Allason
Sir Thomas Arnold
Mr Vivian Bendall
Dr John G. Blackburn
Sir Richard Body
Sir Nicholas Bonsor
Mr Nicholas Budgen
Mr John Butcher
Mr John Carlisle
Mr Michael Carttiss

Mr William Cash
Mr Michael Clark
Mr James Cran
Mr Nirj Joseph Deva
Mr Den Dover
Mr Alan Duncan
Mr Iain Duncan-
  Smith
Mr Nigel Evans
Mr Michael Fabricant
Sir Nicholas Fairbairn
Mr Peter Fry
Mr Phil Gallie
Mr Christopher Gill
Mrs Teresa Gorman
Mr Harry Greenway
Mr John Greenway

Mr Peter Griffiths
Mr Warren Hawksley
Mr Andrew Hunter
Mr Toby Jessel
Mr Roger Knapman
Sir Ivan Lawrence
Mr Barry Legg
Mr Michael Lord
Sir Patrick McNair-
  Wilson
Mr Paul Marland
Mr Tony Marlow
Mr Roger Moate
Sir Michael Neubert
Mr James Pawsey
Mr Barry Porter
Mr David Porter
Mr Andrew Robathan

Mrs Marion Roe
Mr William Ross
Mr David Shaw
Mr Richard Shepherd
Sir Trevor Skeet
Mr Walter Sweeney
Mr John Sykes
Sir Peter Tapsell
Sir Teddy Taylor
Sir Gerard Vaughan
Mr Bill Walker
Mr Gary Waller
Mr John Whittingdale
Mr John Wilkinson
Mrs Ann Winterton
Mr Nicholas
  Winterton

Appendix 2

GDP growth in Germany and UK & UK Money supply

Percentage annual growth
1980 to 1991

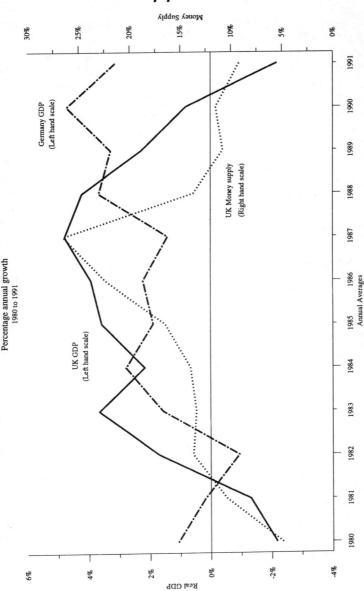

A chart showing how the German and British economies have been on opposite paths but how, in recent years, monetary policy in Britain has related to the requirements of the German economy.

Index